The Intermediate Arche.

Ben Hastings

The Intermediate
ARCHER

Everything They Didn't Tell You
in the Beginner's Course

Meyer & Meyer Sport

British Library of Cataloguing in Publication Data
A catalogue record for this book is available from the British Library

The Intermediate Archer
Maidenhead: Meyer & Meyer Sport (UK) Ltd., 2023
ISBN: 978-1-78255-257-4

© 2023 by Meyer & Meyer Sport (UK) Ltd.
Aachen, Auckland, Beirut, Cairo, Cape Town, Dubai, Hägendorf, Hong Kong, Indianapolis, Maidenhead,
Manila, New Delhi, Singapore, Sydney, Tehran, Vienna
 Member of the World Sport Publishers' Association (WSPA), www.w-s-p-a.org
Printed by Print Consult GmbH, Munich, Germany
Printed in Slovakia.

MIX
Paper from
responsible sources
FSC www.fsc.org   FSC® C084279

ISBN: 978-1-78255-257-4
Email: info@m-m-sports.com
www.thesportspublisher.com

CONTENTS

ACKNOWLEDGMENTS

First and foremost, I have to thank Mike, my coach and mentor in archery, for his encouragement, humour, loan of his notes, and immense technical knowledge. I also need to thank Jane, his lovely wife for feeding me on occasions and being able to endure the endless archery chatter and story-telling—it helps that she is also an archery coach, but she puts up with a lot!

My mother's artistic ability skipped a generation, so original illustrations are the wonderful work of my extremely talented (and beautiful) daughter Saffiyah. She wasn't at all sure of what I wanted, but came up with the perfect style and clarity.

One of the people I coach, Clara, was my model for the colour photographs, and was very keen the moment the possibility was mentioned to her.

Farnham Archers, my club for the past few years, is a great place to shoot, full of a fantastic variety of people, all friendly, engaging, and encouraging, and I have to thank everyone there for helping, advising, and being part of the journey that brought this book into being.

Geoff and Liz at Meyer and Meyer were immediately enthusiastic when this project was mentioned to them.

My long-suffering wife and often archery widow has got used to the idea that the ideal number of bows for an archer to own is $n+1$ where n is the number currently owned. I have to thank her for proofreading the manuscript and also applying her clinical knowledge to much of the anatomy and physiology in the book.

Finally, I would like to thank you for reading it. I hope you find it helpful and encouraging, and that it helps you continue, develop, and progress in archery.

INTRODUCTION

WHO THIS BOOK IS FOR

This book is intended to fill a gap in resources available to archers who have completed a beginner's course and are wondering where they go next. What variety of archery is for them? How can they improve their technique? What sort of equipment should they buy? How much should they spend on it? What bits of equipment are essential right now and which can wait until a few months or a year down the track?

This book is subtitled "Everything They Didn't Tell You in the Beginner's Course," not because I have any reasonable doubt about the quality of courses offered by the vast majority of clubs, but because time on a beginner's course is necessarily limited and the main need for the club is to concentrate first on ensuring you— and everyone around you—are safe and behave safely, and then to concentrate on ensuring the course is enjoyable and fun (this being the key to turning courses into membership fees). You will almost certainly find many things in this book that they did, in fact, teach you on the course. These bear repetition. Some people, in their excitement on the day, may not have heard them or have forgotten them, or just need the extra emphasis. Please don't be insulted by that repetition.

Quite a few archery clubs offer excellent lessons for beginners, whether on a course that takes an hour or so on a Saturday morning for several weeks, or a course that fits into one or two days. Coaching beyond that point is more of a problem since it requires dedication not only from the archer themselves but also from suitably qualified coaches, most of whom give their time for free. Many archery clubs have unqualified archers teaching beginners. This is not necessarily a bad thing—I have met unqualified archers who provide extremely good coaching to a beginner and qualified coaches who shouldn't be allowed anywhere near the field in the first place. All that most beginner's courses teach you is how to shoot safely without endangering yourself, others around you, or the surroundings.

I do not, therefore, intend this book to replace coaching from a qualified club coach. To provide advice on form, technique, and good (and bad) habits requires patient observation, thoughtful analysis, good psychology, and trust in both directions. You can video yourself and watch back what you do—from one angle only. A coach will look at what you are doing from all around—with suitable camera equipment even from above and almost right in front of you. But this book can help you get started. I hope that it will prove a useful companion right up to the point where you are entering competitions and beginning to think about classification status such as Master or Grand Master Bowman.

WHAT IT CONTAINS

What's in this book? Answers to many of the questions that any archer will ask as soon as their beginner's course is over and they have the certificate in their hand allowing them to shoot unsupervised. And that is all that most beginner's courses will do for you. There is little time to provide good coaching on technique, on how to improve results, or even etiquette on the shooting line (although this last item really should have been included).

In here you can find some details on archery equipment suitable for an intermediate archer. For the purposes of this book, my definition of an intermediate archer is being stretched slightly here, to include someone who has only just completed their beginner's course rather than someone who already owns a useful bow with arrows matched to their draw length and the bow's draw weight, and can make necessary adjustments to the equipment themselves.

Almost all references and illustrations in the book are for a right-handed archer (or, more accurately, an archer shooting right-handed). I have nothing whatsoever against "lefties", and I apologise for this apparent bias, but being totally inclusive and thus having to explain each time which way things go could easily cause confusion. Where there might be a difference I make an effort to explain this.

Archery uses quite a mixture of units. Most of this is a matter of history. You will find many weights measured in pounds or kilograms, distances in yards or metres, target sizes (generally) in centimetres, bow lengths usually in inches, stabiliser weights might be in ounces or grams, bow equipment threads could be metric or imperial. This can get confusing, and sometimes care needs to be taken to avoid financial loss in ordering the wrong item or damaging equipment by trying to force the wrong size bolt into a hole.

There are several different disciplines within archery. If you don't like being cold, wet, and muddy, then indoor target archery is probably the area for you. Combining a walk (or run) in the woods carrying everything you might need during the day with shooting at distances you have to gauge for yourself at either formal paper targets or models of animals, then 3D or field archery might tickle your fancy. The majority of this book, however, is going to concentrate mostly on target archery, whether indoor or outdoor, on a regulated range.

That still leaves quite a few variations on the theme. Olympic recurve (or freestyle)—a recurve bow with damping, stabilisation, a sight, and a draw-length indicator (clicker)—is probably the most common form of club archery. Barebow—similar to freestyle but without any aids to sighting, stabilisation, or damping—is slowly becoming more popular. It provides additional challenges in technique which I will touch on later. Compound bows offer technological assistance in holding a powerful and very accurate bow at full draw through the assistance of cams and cables. Once again, more information will be found in the relevant chapter. One of the other bow forms you will often see on an outdoor range is a traditional bow such as a flatbow or longbow. Longbows in particular tend to have much heavier draw weights and so are not really suitable for a raw beginner, but after technique and upper body fitness have improved, longbows can offer a lot to someone who likes the feeling of participating in and re-enacting the heyday of archery from mediaeval through to Tudor times.

WHY JOIN A CLUB?

There is no compulsion whatsoever to join an archery club. If you prefer solitude, shoot in your back garden or elsewhere on private property without others to distract you; you don't need to spend money on either club fees or national association subscriptions. You would, however, be well advised to have some form of insurance against third-party accidents. You also need to ensure that others can't stray into the path of your arrows and that, should a misfire or equipment failure send an arrow in an unusual direction, suitable barriers such as good stop netting will protect your legal and financial status. Please don't be tempted to shoot on public land without either permission or extensive precautions against accident and injury.

All that said, I heartily recommend joining a club. Apart from the obvious social benefits, a club is where you're most likely to find someone to coach you for free or where, if you need a metal detector to look for that arrow which went astray or the loan of one of the rarer and more expensive tools such as an arrow jack, one will be available to borrow. Other archers will almost always be happy to give you the benefit of their experience, to show you their equipment, and allow you to try out their bows or other equipment. A club will have insurance, maintain the range, hold a (usually small) stock of target faces and pins, and keep its members notified of events, upcoming competitions whether internal, regional, or national, and encourage improvement and development of technique and results. Other club members will help with maintenance of your equipment, such as loaning you a fletching jig, teaching you how to refletch or repoint arrows, or tuning your set-up. They will also often have second-hand equipment they want to get rid of—often at discount prices; my own club organises a sort of archery jumble sale regularly! For those archers who want to advance their classification, clubs will organise suitable events and maintain records of scores and resultant classifications. I can sum up what membership of a club provides in one word—support.

WHEN TO BUY

Not now, if you can help it. Don't rush it. Archery can be an expensive hobby and while a particular bit of kit may suit you right now, you don't want to spend loads of money on it only to find you outgrow it in either physical size, strength, ability, or technique in only a few months. Some clubs will lend or hire equipment. There are organisations out there which will hire equipment, often quite cheaply. One such in the UK is Stylist Bows near Rugby in Warwickshire, another is Urban Archers (see the Links section at the end of the book).

For younger juniors, aged up to about 13 or 14, I would not normally recommend renting a bow since very few rental bows are suitable for the youngest archers. Buy an inexpensive takedown bow instead. Alternatively, some clubs have bows available to borrow.

For older archers, if the rental option is not available, I don't recommend spending huge sums on the "best" equipment. Do some research on the internet, as people often outgrow bows and sell onwards. Get advice on items from someone experienced in your club (see above!). Above all, bear in mind that as your technique and your upper body fitness improve you will need different equipment. At time of writing, a basic wooden takedown bow can be bought for £55 in the UK, and limbs start at around £35. More advanced risers (the central part of a recurve bow) can go up to £800 new. A pair of more advanced limbs will set you back anything from £100–800. There is no shame whatsoever in starting out with basic equipment; everyone was an inexperienced beginner once, and nobody really wants to waste money. Nor is there any shame whatsoever in going to an archery supplies shop and asking for advice and trying out different combinations of equipment. If the shop won't let you try things out, go to another shop. Above all, don't rush into anything. A good riser will last you years—you don't want one that's wrong for you.

There is more information for the prospective buyer in the chapter on equipment.

COACHING

You are unlikely to proceed or improve much without coaching. It is possible to improve through watching videos online or posting photos and videos in online groups, but it is much harder, and you get little feedback even when you can separate the good advice from the bad.

Get a coach.

If your club doesn't have a suitable coach—and some don't—find a club which does. Some coaches will charge for their services, particularly those who operate outside the normal club structure. Note that an outside coach will most probably not be allowed to coach at your club without paying for associate membership as a minimum. Most coaching within a club is provided free of charge—although most coaches will always appreciate the occasional token of appreciation!

A good coach will observe and examine your style and technique; suggest priorities for what to address first; provide feedback on progress; suggest off-line activities to improve your technique, strength, and stamina; help, listen, encourage, solve problems, suggest goals, advise, raise awareness, be non-judgemental, and challenge. Oh—and console when it doesn't go right!

The relationship between you and your coach should, first and foremost, be one of trust and honesty. They will ask you questions such as "How much have you been practising the past week?" If the real answer is that you haven't been to the range once, say so. Don't say "Oh, a few times." Believe me, they'll be able to tell as soon as they see you shoot!

If there is any sort of reticence or other problem between you and your coach, talk it out. If you can't resolve the problem, change coaches. Interpersonal difficulties are part of life, and the coach will understand. Don't accept coaching from someone else without first clearing it with your present coach.

And finally, in order to know more about what to expect from a coach, you can download Archery GB's Code of Conduct for Coaches at the link provided at the end of the book.

CHAPTER 1

A BRIEF HISTORY OF ARCHERY

Half a million years ago, humans used sticks with fire-hardened points as spears. Spears became javelins, but it is quite a long step from there to propelling the spear by using a mechanical aid.

INVENTION OF ARCHERY

"MAN, I REALLY WANT TO STAB THAT GUY, BUT HE'S WAY OVER THERE."

imgflip.com

The first known use of fire by our ancestors was over a million years ago. The earliest archaeological evidence of starting a fire by friction is dated to approximately 4,000 BCE in Triquet Island, British Columbia. I had hoped in my research to find that use of bow drills to make fire predated use of bows as weapons, but, sadly for me, the earliest arrows appear to predate bow drills, dating from around 60,000 years ago in Africa. My hope was that one day whilst making fire with a bow drill, the shaft slipped and twanged out of the bow, giving the operator a sudden burst of inspiration! But no. Outside Africa, until about 2020, the earliest known arrowheads dated to about 46,000 BCE and were found in a cave in Sri Lanka. Since then, however, arrowheads (this is awaiting confirmation as I write this) dating back to 52,000 BCE have been found in Grotte Mandrin cave in the Rhône Valley.

It might be a fair assumption to state that use of bows for hunting predated bows as war weapons, but having decided that using a bow to bring down animals for food was a good idea, it can't have been a terribly long step from there to realising that a bow could also be used to stop other people hunting what you regarded as your legitimate food store, or to raid other people's stores of food.

However it was that use of the bow developed, it would have taken a huge step to go from using purely muscle power in order to propel a missile to storing energy and releasing it suddenly—and faster and more efficiently—and thus more effectively. It also meant, of course, that the hunter (or primitive soldier) could stay farther away from the prey (or enemy). It did, however, require some expertise and familiarity with the right materials, with how to make a bow, the string, arrowheads, and shafts, and this is technology which Neanderthals did not appear to possess. Ultimately, this may have contributed to their being out-evolved.

Spears, of course, predated arrows and were already equipped with bone, horn, or stone tips, so using those on arrows was an obvious next step where the source materials were available.

Bows as weapons for hunting and war are found in history throughout the world, from North and South America to North and East Africa, throughout Europe, India, Sri Lanka, China, Japan, and the Andaman and Solomon Islands although, interestingly, not in Australasia.

Cave paintings depicting scenes of hunting with bows and arrows have been found in Spain at Vilafranca in Castellón, Spain. Dating to approximately 5,000 BCE, they include drawings of two aurochs, two human archers, and a goat. From a similar period, the Cave of Archers is a rock art shelter of the Gilf Kebir National Park in the New Valley Governorate, Egypt. The rock paintings feature a few people with bows and arrows as well as a herd of bovine animals—possibly cows, possibly aurochs.

Around 2,300 BCE, bodies were buried in southern England at Stonehenge, Amesbury, and Boscombe Down with grave goods that strongly suggest the deceased were archers. The Stonehenge Archer appears to have been deliberately and carefully buried in a ditch. Aged around 30 and apparently killed by arrows, the man came to be called an archer because of the stone wrist guard, or bracer, and several flint arrowheads buried with him. The Amesbury Archer is so called because of having been buried with not only several barbed stone arrow heads but also two wrist guards.

There was also a wealth of other grave goods, including funerary pots, copper knives, metalworking and flint-knapping tools, and the oldest known worked gold objects in the country. The Boscombe Bowmen also had arrowheads buried with them. The grave contained seven bodies: three men, and four younger bodies, who appear to have been related to each other. One man was buried in a crouched position with the bones of the others scattered around him, and their skulls at his feet.

During the Trojan War (around 12th or 13th century BCE), Homer describes Philoctetes and Odysseus as highly accomplished archers, and legend states that Achilles was killed by a poisoned arrow shot by Paris. Odysseus proved his identity to his wife Penelope by stringing his war bow, a feat of which nobody else was rumoured to be capable, and shooting an arrow through ten axehead rings. Whether these figures were fictional or not we can't, of course, know, but clearly Homer was familiar with archery as a technique of hunting and war.

In what is now modern-day Greece, at the Battle of Thermopylae in 480 BCE, the Spartan leader Leonidas is reported to have been advised to surrender with the warning by the Persians that their arrows would fly so thickly they would obscure the sun. Leonidas' answer is reported by Herodotus to have welcomed the ability to fight in the shade.

Different cultures, different terrain, and different methods of warfare resulted in very differing styles of equipment and technique. Asian warriors were often mounted on horseback, thus shorter composite bows became popular in order to be able to swing the bow across the horse's neck to shoot on the other side or over the animal's haunches. In much of Europe, crossbows were popular, while longbows—generally made of a wood such as yew, ash, or elm, and which probably were first used by Welsh archers, and adopted and adapted by the English—made England a military power in Europe (particularly France) through much of the Middle Ages.

Henry III's Assize of Arms (1252) required all "citizens, burgesses, free tenants, villeins and others from 15 to 60 years of age" to be armed. At minimum, they were required to own a halberd and a knife. Those who owned land valued at more than £2 also had to own a bow, thus making the raising of an army both easier and cheaper.

Longbows were decisive in battles such as Sluys (1340), Crécy (1346), Poitiers (1356), and Agincourt (1415). They were less successful at later battles as you will see later in this chapter.

The Battle of Sluys, a sea battle between English and French ships, resembled a land engagement at sea. Two opposing ships would be lashed together and the men-at-arms would then engage in hand-to-hand fighting while supporting troops fired arrows or bolts.

King Edward III sent his ships against the French fleet in units of three (two ships carrying archers flanking one with men-at-arms). The English ships with the archers would approach a French ship and loose arrows at a rate of more than ten per minute from each archer onto its decks; the men-at-arms would then board and take the vessel. Longbow historian Robert Hardy believed that the English archers with longbows had a rate of fire two or three times greater than the French crossbowmen and significantly outranged them, and that the longbows had an effective range of 300 yards compared with 200 yards for the crossbows.

It is quite possible that English weather may have made longbows more popular than crossbows since in wet weather a longbow with a hemp bowstring can easily and quickly be unstrung and the string protected from damp and the resultant stretching if it gets wet, or replaced with another, while crossbows cannot. This was a significant feature of the Battle of Crécy, to the advantage of the English army, when the mercenary Genoese crossbowmen found they lost all power from their bows having been unable to unstring them in a brief shower early on in the battle.

At the Battle of Poitiers (1356), fully a third of the army under the Black Prince were English and Welsh longbowmen. At Agincourt, Henry V had approximately 7,000 archers under Sir Thomas Erpingham, and only about 1,500 men-at-arms.

In 1388 it was ordered by Richard II that "no servants in husbandry, or labourer, shall wear any sword, buckler, or dagger." The same act prohibited "unlawful" games and specified that all such servants, labourers, husbandmen, victuallers, and artificers were to have bows and to practise on Sundays and holy days.

An Act of 1465 specified "that every Englishman and Irishman that dwelleth with Englishmen, and speaketh English, betwixt sixty and sixteen in years, shall have an English bow and arrows."

Various acts specified that any ship importing any goods into England also had to bring bow staves or finished bows. In 1487 there was "an Acte against the excessive price of Longe bowes" which set a maximum price for bows of 3s 6d; I have yet to discover if this has since been repealed!

There is an urban myth that a law was passed making it legal to shoot a Welshman in the City of Chester, and that this law has never been repealed.

During the Battle of Shrewsbury in 1403—after Welsh uprisings in and around Chester, and the defection of Sir Henry "Hotspur" Percy to join forces with Owain Glyndwr—Prince Henry of Monmouth (the future King Henry V) was wounded in the face by an arrow which left him with a permanent scar. He decreed that there should be a curfew on Welshmen in Chester:

"...all manner of Welsh persons or Welsh sympathies should be expelled from the city; that no Welshman should enter the city before sunrise or tarry in it after sunset, under pain of decapitation."

Welshmen were required to leave their weapons at the town gates and not congregate in groups of three or more. A few years later in 1408, the citizens of Chester elected a Welshman, John Ewloe, as mayor. Chester had no argument with the Welsh and, sadly, I have to report that this urban myth is no more than that.

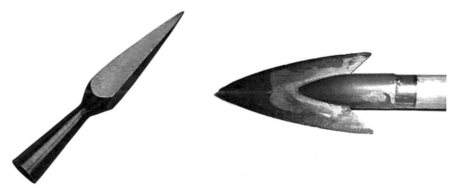

Bodkin and broadhead arrowheads

Arrowheads were usually either bodkins, a square cross-section type of narrow steel point, which could pierce armour at close range, or broadheads, which were frequently barbed and had sharpened blades to cause as much injury and bleeding as possible to relatively unprotected targets on both entry and removal. The effective range of a longbow was anything from a few yards up to around 220 yards. In practice, of course, effective range was considerably more than in battle as the rate of fire was not as demanding, the food was better, and the archers were not tired by days (or weeks) of marching in poor weather with little night-time shelter.

A longbow was a difficult weapon to master. It took ten years to build the strength and ability to draw the heaviest bows, practising for at least an hour per week. Professional bowmen soldiers (as opposed to conscripts) would practise more. They were expected to be able to shoot between five and ten arrows a minute, both high in trajectory and directly at the enemy, and to keep that performance up for several hours.

Longbows were extremely effective when the army had time to prepare the ground in advance of action. This preparation would normally include setting stakes, digging holes to catch horses' hooves, and using as much water as possible to soften the earth. They were in trouble, however, when there was no time to prepare since bowmen were only lightly armoured and had little in the way of self-defence. Thus at the battles of Pontvallain (1370), Verneuil (1424), and Patay (1429), the longbowmen were completely routed. It is, perhaps, not entirely surprising that little is taught in British school history classes about those battles!

There were several statutes issued in England mandating the manufacture, import, and keeping of arms throughout the Middle Ages—not all of them very successful. Evidence is ubiquitous of the importance of archery to the defence of the country (and offence in others!). One is the preponderance of yew trees in old churchyards. Yew is poisonous to many animals and, as grazing land was open in the Middle Ages, the only enclosed spaces were churchyards. Thus the local churchyard was the only space safe to cultivate yew without endangering grazing herds. Another indicator of the importance to England of archery is the number of archery-related surnames such as Bowman, Archer, Bowyer, Stringer, Stringfellow, Arrowsmith, and Fletcher.

While no longbows of the Mediaeval period survive, we have over 130 bows recovered from the wreck of the Mary Rose, Henry VIII's navy's flagship which sank off Portsmouth in 1545, during the declining years of the longbow's career as a weapon of war in Europe.

We have only estimates for the draw weight of longbows of the time, since it is not known what effects aging had on the wood—let alone centuries of submersion and burial had on the bows from Mary Rose. However, for comparison, a modern longbow is usually 60 lbs maximum, which is comparable to hunting (rather than war) bows of the period. However, estimates of the Mary Rose's bows vary from 80 or 90 lbs up to 185 lbs.

Naturally, no archer would have been able to pull a 180 lb bow without considerable training and working gradually up to that. Draw technique is very different from a modern recurve bow, but skeletons of men believed to have been archers from the period show significant deformation.

In central Asia, tribesmen became very adept at archery from horseback. This required a horsebow which was shorter than a European longbow; in order to reach the power needed, horsebows were generally made from a composite of materials rather than a single stave of wood. The use of the bow frequently identified the enemy in the minds of citizens of states like the Chinese Han, who called their neighbours "Those who draw the bow."

Increasing use of gunpowder in warfare made the bow as a war weapon obsolete and archery soon became a sport. Although the first-known archery competition was held in Finsbury, England, in 1583 with a remarkable field of 3,000 participants, it wasn't until the late 18th century that it started to become more popular.

The Toxophilite Society was formed in London in 1781, under the patronage of the Prince of Wales, the future Prince Regent and King George IV. However, at this stage archery was more a recreation than a sport, and one reserved to the nobility and landed gentry.

The first Grand National Archery Society (GNAS, the predecessor of Archery GB) meeting was held in York in 1844 and over the next decade, rules were standardized as the York Round—a series of shoots with six dozen arrows shot at 100 yards, four at 80 yards, and two at 60 yards. The mathematicians among you will quickly work that out as totalling twelve dozen arrows—144 arrows each scoring a maximum possible of 10. The perfect score of 1440 is the key to working out handicaps and their application.

Another popular urban myth concerns "Mad Jack" Churchill, a British Army officer who took his Scottish broadsword, bagpipes, and several longbows to war with him in France in 1939. The myth states that Churchill killed a German soldier with his longbow in an attack on a German patrol near L'Épinette in the Pas de Calais.

However, it is only a myth. Churchill himself later stated that his bows had been destroyed earlier in the campaign when they were crushed by a lorry.

Archery first featured in the second modern Olympic Games in 1900. While traditional ("primitive") archery experienced a form of revival in the United States in the early 20th century, it has mostly been modern forms of archery which have survived and now flourish, with the development of the modern recurve bow and compound bows. Archery returned to the Olympic Games in 1972. However, large communities of archers shooting traditional bows such as longbows, American flatbows, and horsebows still remain active today.

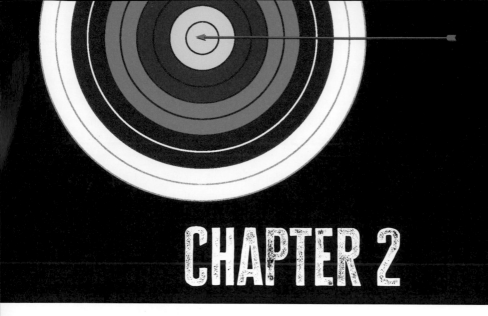

CHAPTER 2

ARCHERY TYPES

Much of this book concerns target archery, since this is the area in which most archers start their career and is the predominant form of archery across the world. However, it is very far from the only discipline which exists, and there is a very rich seam that can be explored from cultures across the world and history, as I hope I showed in the previous chapter. I cover different types of bows in the next chapter.

TARGET ARCHERY

This can itself be subdivided, but is dominated by recurve bows. It can be shot both indoors and out, with different rules for each form of competition.

Modern competitive target archery is governed by the World Archery Federation (WA), formerly Fédération Internationale de Tir à l'Arc (FITA). WA is the International Olympic Committee's (IOC) recognised governing body for all of archery. Olympic rules derive from WA rules.

Target archery consists largely in arrows being shot in a series of ends—normally six at a time outdoors and three indoors—at a target a set distance away from the archers who are at a line on the ground called the shooting line. The target can vary in size and format depending on the event and distance, but almost all are a series of rings, gold in the centre, then red, blue, black, and white on the outer edge. The usual target sizes and distances (and events generally using them) are:

➤ 40 cm at 18 m WA Indoor Compound
➤ 60 cm at 18 m WA Indoor Recurve
➤ 80 cm at 30 and 50 m WA
➤ 122 cm at 70 and 90 m WA

Your beginner's course will most likely have used 122 cm target faces.

There are different rounds consisting of different numbers of arrows shot at different distances and a competition organiser will announce in advance what format the competition will take. These rounds are normally open to freestyle (Olympic recurve), barebow, longbow, and compound archers. Rounds are specified in the rules of shooting (see the Links section at the end of this book).

In Great Britain, Imperial rounds, measured in yards, are still used for many tournaments and these have slightly different rules to metric (WA) rounds, which are used internationally. Archers are divided into seniors and juniors, with juniors being those under the age of 18. Some competitions will have further subdivision of archers by age.

FIELD ARCHERY

Field archery is governed by the International Field Archery Association (IFAA).

Field archers are required to be able to shoot without knowing—but visually assessing—the distance to the target, some of which can be longer than in target archery. They shoot with a group of others away from rivals in an imitation of hunting situations. Targets are located at varying distances from the archers in rough terrain. There are further challenges such as coping with the weather and changing light and wind.

There are three forms of rounds: hunter, animal, and field. In a hunter round, the distances of the targets from the archer vary as far as 60m. The target has an all-black face with a white or yellow centre. For animal rounds, life-sized 2D pictures of animals as targets are used with scores depending on hitting vital or nonvital zones. Finally, the field round is similar to target archery with targets laid out at set distances using target faces with a black inner ring, two white middle rings, and two black outer rings.

Archers can be required to shoot both uphill and down, so the archer will need to practise in various positions, sometimes with unsure footing or among obstructions to foot placement and visual or bow obstructions. Shooting up and downhill gives the added complication of calculating angles because of gravity—something a target archer is not bothered about.

There are multiple classes (recognised types) of bows including American flatbow, barebow, bowhunter, compound limited, freestyle, hunting tackle, longbow, primitive, traditional bowhunter, unlimited, and crossbow.

Competitor divisions are

»→ recurve and compound,
»→ barebow, cadet recurve, and cadet compound, and
»→ cadet barebow.

Each of these will shoot from different distances to each target, marked by red, blue, and yellow pegs or stakes, respectively. Frequently, further divisions are allowed for juniors.

A full course is normally 24 targets with competitors shooting three arrows at each target. During the course of a shoot, an archer must be prepared to carry everything they might need with them, in pockets, in a quiver, or in a backpack. They must also be prepared to conduct running repairs in the event of equipment malfunction, so a small toolkit might well be needed.

3D ARCHERY

3D archery is similar in many respects to field archery, in that it is conducted over a course of often rough terrain, in whatever weather is provided on the day! The main difference is that no 2D targets are used. Targets may be hard foam models of animal or other items such as drinks cans or bottles, and may be life-size or not, giving added difficulty to gauging distances to the targets.

There are scoring rings on the animal that correspond to different scores. Different types of rounds have different systems of scoring, depending where on the animal is hit, and the score is reduced if more than one arrow is required to hit the target.

The number of arrows shot will depend on the competition, and can vary—it can be just one arrow per target or two or three depending on each tournament's rules. Courses are normally 36 or 40 targets and each archer is allowed up to 3 shots at the target if it is not hit first time, so an archer could shoot up to 120 arrows.

CLOUT ARCHERY

In clout archery, archers shoot arrows at a flag (clout) from a relatively long distance at a high trajectory, scoring depending on how close each arrow lands to the flag. Each arrow scores points for the scoring zone in which it enters the ground. An arrow embedded in the flagpole counts highest. An arrow lying on the ground is considered to be in the scoring zone in which its point lies.

A tournament typically consists of a double clout round, with a total of six dozen arrows being shot.

The English Longbow Society has its own rules for clout shooting. Archers are restricted to the use of English longbows and wooden arrows. Ladies shoot at 120 yards, gentlemen at 180 yards. Instead of a flag, the target is a 30" diameter white circle, on a frame at 45 degrees to the ground with a 4" central black spot. Concentric rings are marked at 30", 4 feet, 7 feet, 10 feet, and 13 feet from the centre. Scoring is 6 for a clout, down to 1 for the outside ring. Two rounds of 36 arrows in 12 ends of 3 are shot to make a double clout round.

World Archery Clout shoots differ again in that the target flag consists of a piece of coloured fabric 80cm high and 30 cm wide on a softwood pole, with the flag 50 cm from the ground.

HORSE ARCHERY

Horse archery is another method of linking yourself back to traditional forms of archery. In its origins, it was the usual method of hunting, protecting the herds, and making war. It was practised by a huge swathe of races across Europe and Asia, including:

≫• Eurasian nomads
≫• Alans

- Scythians
- Sarmatians
- Parthians
- Sassanid Persians
- Indians
- Hungarians
- Mongols
- Chinese
- Turkic peoples
- Huns
- Mesopotamians
- Japanese (yabusame)

"Having neither cities nor forts, and carrying their dwellings with them wherever they go; accustomed, moreover, one and all of them, to shoot from horseback; and living not by husbandry but on their cattle, their wagons the only houses that they possess, how can they fail of being unconquerable, and unassailable even?" (Herodotus on the Scythians)

Horse archery also developed separately in the Americas. In the North American prairies, following the introduction of domesticated horses to the continent, the Comanches were especially skilled.

Since using a bow requires the rider to let go of the reins completely, horse archers need excellent equestrian skills to be able to shoot effectively on the move, while controlling the horse only with their knees. The need to shoot on either side, forwards, or backwards also dictates that for manoeuvrability the bow needs to be short, and the quiver must not prevent swinging the bow; thus many horse quivers are back-mounted.

It should also be obvious that the horse needs to be trained specifically for archery and there needs to be a good understanding between the archer/rider and the horse.

Horse archery was revived in Mongolia after independence in 1921. However, despite its history and the record of Mongolian horse archers, the sport is very limited in Mongolia itself. The Mongolian Horseback Archery Association has competed in South Korea and Europe.

Horse archery is a growing sport in the United States, with horse archery clubs around the country. Competitive courses incorporate the Korean, Hungarian, and Persian Styles. Riders run reinless down a 90-meter course while loosing arrows at various target arrangements.

The British Horseback Archery Association is the governing body of horse archery in the UK, and held the first national competition in 2010. Since 2013, members have represented Great Britain in international team competitions. Encouragingly, categories for disabled riders and for juniors have also been introduced.

The life and work of Kassai Lajos, who created the competitive rule system of horse archery in the late 1980s, was dramatized by Géza Kaszás in a 2016 film *A Lovasíjász (The Horse Archer).*

POPINJAY ARCHERY

This is, to my mind, one of the weirder forms of archery. The object of popinjay archery is to knock artificial birds off their perches. The perches are cross-pieces on top of a 90-foot mast. The "cock" (the largest bird) is set on the top cross piece. Four smaller "hens" are set on the next crosspiece down. Two dozen or so "chicks" (the smallest birds) are set on the lower cross pieces. (See the figure on the following page.) This reputedly descends from the practice used by longbowmen on board ship; in order to maintain their skill, feather clusters were placed on the yardarms and at the top of the mast.

You will quickly gather that the archers shoot close to vertical for best results—shelter has to be provided for archers other than the shooter! (Only one archer can shoot at a time.) Only arrows with blunt tips (0.75"–1" diameter) may be used. Points are scored for knocking the "birds" off their perches, the cock scoring 5 points, the hens 3 points, and the chicks 1 point.

OTHERS

Archery GB rules allow for archery golf and archery darts, but at time of writing I don't know any clubs which operate these!

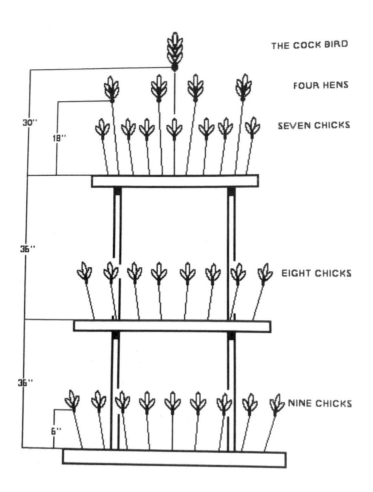

THE COCK BIRD

FOUR HENS

SEVEN CHICKS

EIGHT CHICKS

NINE CHICKS

30" 18" 36" 36" 6"

CHAPTER 3

BOW TYPES

ARCHER'S PARADOX

You'll hear a lot about Archer's Paradox. What is it? Well, firstly, it is NOT that an arrow in flight wobbles and bends; the wobble and bend is, partly, how the arrow overcomes archer's paradox.

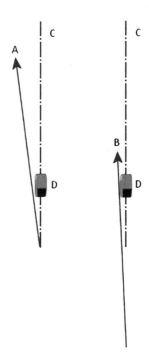

When nocked on the bow, an arrow points in a direction that is completely different from the path it will take when it is shot, and this is the paradox. Here's a diagram of a recurve or longbow.

In the diagram, it can be seen that when nocked, the arrow points well off to the left (for a right-handed archer) towards A. When drawn, it points more to the right, towards B. The actual flight of the arrow is at the target, C. D is the riser.

The reason the arrow departs the bow towards C is physics—the impulse to the arrow comes from the string at the base of the arrow, while the bulk of the mass, which gives the inertia, is at the front of the arrow, in the pile. Therefore the arrow's first reaction to being given a kick up the backside is for the end to move and the front to stay where it is, so it bends in the middle. The point and centre of the arrow are more static, one through inertia, the other by the plunger button, and the nock end slides off the archer's fingers moving slightly to the left in the case of a right-handed archer, so the end of the arrow swings away from the bow. Then, since the plunger button is set to one side, the arrow bends in the other direction. This sets up an oscillation in the shaft, which bends first one way then the other, but the direction of flight is that in which the impetus from the string hit it—straight at the target. And the reason is that the oscillation is about the nodes of the arrow (the points on the shaft which stay still when the rest of it is flexing), which continue to fly straight whatever the rest of the arrow is doing.

The job of the fletches is to calm down the oscillation and straighten the flight so that by the time it arrives at the target, the shaft is straight and it is, we hope, following exactly the same flight path as the previous arrow.

OLYMPIC RECURVE

As can be seen in the figure, both limbs curve first one way, then the other. Therefore, as it is drawn, the section of the limb closest to the riser will bend more and then the outer section will straighten.

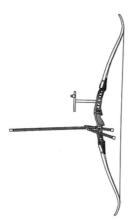
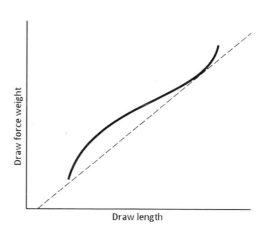

The draw weight of a longbow increases in almost a straight line. For a recurve bow, the curve is close to a straight line (see diagram). Initially, as the longer sections of the limbs bend, the draw force increases steadily, then begins to tail off. The draw weight, however, increases again significantly as the recurved limb sections straighten the further the string is drawn. The nominal specified draw weight is measured at 28" draw. Someone with a shorter draw will find less weight on the fingers, and a longer draw results in a heavier pull on the fingers.

The limbs are easily removed from the riser for storage or for exchanging for another set of limbs, either lighter or heavier draw weight. The riser incorporates a grip section which in many models is removable or adjustable depending on the archer's hand shape, size, and physiology. There are also mounting points for a sight, clicker, arrow rest, and stabilisers.

Various different specifications exist for types of mounting limbs, the most common being International Limb Fitting (ILF).

The specifications for an Olympic recurve bow are laid down by the Archery Trade Association (ATA), formerly called the Archery Manufacturers' Organization (AMO), which exists to ensure consistent standards and stringent guidelines across different manufacturers' products.

COMPOUND

A compound bow uses a system of cams, cables, and wheels to provide a means of reducing the load on the archer at full draw. Therefore, when at full draw, the peak weight of the bow is reduced or let off (you will hear the term "in the valley"). The initial draw weight is high, reaching a peak at about mid-draw until the let-off zone, when the weight on the archer's pull reduces. The amount of the let-off varies from one bow to another.

This provides a way of having a very accurate bow with high power limbs which is still comfortable for the archer to hold at full draw.

The limbs don't detach in normal use, nor does the archer unstring the bow when it is not in use. It is therefore stored fully strung in a case or bag specifically designed for compound bows. The limbs are much shorter than those of a recurve bow.

The bow is most usually shot not off the fingers as a recurve bow is, but using a release aid which clips onto a D-loop on the string behind the arrow nock and which releases the string (mechanisms vary) on demand from the archer.

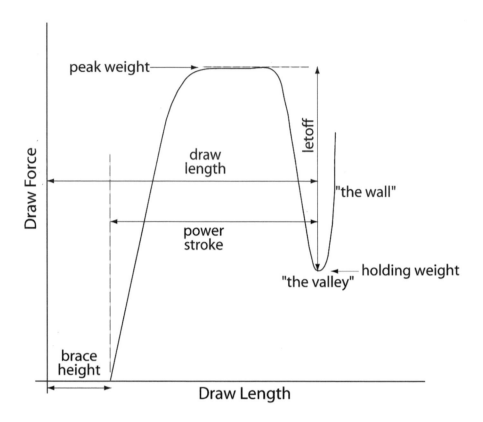

Draw length for a compound bow is usually limited to about 2" either way. This can be changed, but only by changing cams and/or wheels. The draw weight is also difficult to change. To do almost any work on the bow requires it to be put into a bow press to take the load off the limbs safely.

Compound bows are much shorter than recurve bows, and require less stabilisation. You will typically find a compound bow sporting a shorter long rod and sometimes a rear stabiliser rod on the same side as the archer (left for a right-handed archer). Physically, compound bows are heavier in the hand than recurve bows.

Instead of an arrow rest, a compound bow employs a launcher which might be a circle with brushes, or drop-away, or a pair of leaves, one on either side of the shaft. Whichever version is used, arrows for compound bows are fletched differently. For recurve bows, the index fletch is on one side of the shaft, perpendicular to the string groove in the nock, while for compound bows the index fletch is in the same alignment as the groove. The launcher sits in the same plane as the string and the centre-shot setting is neutral—the point of the arrow sits directly behind the string. For this reason, the oscillation of the arrow caused by Archer's Paradox is not fishtailing as it is for a recurve bow but moving vertically, in a porpoising motion.

Sights for a compound bow are also different from those of a recurve bow. A magnifying sight is allowed for compound bows, and a peep sight—basically a circle of metal with a hole in it—is tied into the string at an angle so that it aligns with the archer's eye when the bow is fully drawn. The peep sight and the magnifying sight should work together for you, so fitting the right size peep sight in the right place on the string is something that you will definitely need help with from an experienced compound archer or bow retailer. Bear in mind that the greater the magnification of the sight, the more the picture will appear to wobble, and the less of the whole picture will be visible at full draw, so too great a magnification might actually make it harder to find your aiming point on the target face.

Being shorter than recurve bows and having the need for a release aid, compound bows are very popular with disabled archers, particularly wheelchair users, since the bow is less likely to foul the wheel of the chair. Release aids can be modified or manufactured to suit all sorts of disabilities.

BAREBOW

Barebow archers generally use a recurve bow. The riser is often simply an Olympic recurve but risers are available specifically for barebow use with weight mounting points below the grip that differ from an Olympic recurve riser.

The rules for barebow competition state that no sights, stabilisation, draw length indication (clicker), or damping is permitted, and the whole bow must be capable of fitting when unstrung through a 12.2 cm ring.

Technique is different for barebow archers in that they don't normally shoot split-fingered (one finger above the arrow and two below on the string) but three under (i.e., all three fingers of the draw hand below the arrow). Thus a tab for barebow does not need a slit in the middle of the leather for the arrow shaft.

The archer uses the arrow point to sight on the target, depending on range distance, using techniques called face- or string-walking. Thus a variety of methods exist for sighting and changing procedure, bow set-up, or arrows for different distances.

Sometimes the archer will simply move the arrow point on the target so that it is pointing at the top of the target or the bottom, or at something close to the target—a version of gap aiming—or positioning their string hand so that there is a larger or smaller gap between their index finger and the nocking point (string-walking), or the archer will also change the reference point for their string hand on their face (face-walking). The first place barebow archers will generally learn to use for an anchor point is with their index finger in the corner of their mouth. This might move up for shorter ranges or down for longer, as far as under the chin for the furthest distances, providing that a consistent point can be found such as the jawbone or cheekbone.

In string-walking, the rules provide for limited marking of the face of the archer's tab, so it is generally possible to keep the amount of crawl down the string consistent from one arrow to the next. I should perhaps mention that the centre serving of the string must be just one colour and unmarked, nor should it extend far enough above the nocking point that it can be seen at full draw and thus used as an aiming aid.

So for string-walking, shooting three under and putting the arrow point on the centre of the target, the arrow will hit high on the target at short range. This will, of course, lower as the range increases until you get to a range at which the arrow hits the centre. This is your point on distance. Then for different distances, the crawl on the string will vary—if arrows hit low, then decrease the crawl.

As you will rapidly come to realise, arrow length will make a difference to the amount of crawl or face-walking that a barebow archer will require. A longer arrow will appear to be higher up the target when at full draw than a shorter one, so archers sometimes use different arrows for different distances. This will affect the bow tuning, so they will also use either an easily adjustable button or will swap buttons for another which is already preset for the required tune.

The longer the crawl when string-walking, the more off-centre on the string the archer's draw hand is at full draw. This puts significantly more strain on the limbs, particularly the lower limb, and a barebow will be noisier than an Olympic recurve. This is because at the moment of release, there is a lot of slackness in the lower part of the string while the limb is accelerating, and this is called the dry fire zone. This also throws the tuning of the bow off, and it is impossible to tune a barebow correctly for all distances. Therefore most barebow archers will tune the system for a middle distance and accept the amount it is off-tune at extremes of range.

TRADITIONAL

Traditional bows are, as the name suggests, traditional in construction and materials. Traditional competition is seen by its adherents as the purest form of archery! There are two different types of bow acceptable in traditional competitions, the longbow and the flatbow (often called an American flatbow).

Like barebow, no stabilizers, counterbalances, or weights of any kind are permitted, the only exception being a bow-mounted quiver. The bow has no sight, no markings which might be used to help in sighting are allowed on the bow or the string, and no clicker may be used.

No artificial materials can be used on the bow with the exceptions of the string material and glue, and no performance-enhancing materials can be used to back the bow such as another wood, bamboo, rawhide, or sinew—only decorative materials can be used.

Arrows must be wood, bamboo, or cane, fletched only with natural feathers between 2" and 6" long. They must have at least two and up to six fletches, and a set of arrows must be identical in piles, weight, length, and fletching.

The bow is shot with a glove, finger tab, or bare fingers. Archers are allowed to use up to two nock locators (e.g., thread tied on the string), but they must use the same nocking point and anchor point for each shot and the index finger must contact the string at the same place for each shot. The index finger must touch the nock of the arrow. Face-walking, fixed crawl, and string-walking are not permitted.

Longbows

Longbows can be made either from one piece of wood or composite. They are typically made with a D-shaped cross-section, and are shot from a glove or finger tab. The traditional wood for making longbows was yew. At one point in the late 16th century, yew trees were almost extinct because of the demand for staves to make longbows. A mixture of other woods can be used for longbows, but in general does not perform as well as a yew bow.

The draw weight of modern longbows is generally high—there are bows available at around 25 lbs draw weight, but they are few and far between. It is possible to use modern arrows with a longbow, but the practice is frowned on—be prepared to be ostracised if you try this! Note also that arrows used in competition must be wooden.

Selfbows

A selfbow is a type of longbow made using only one piece of wood, so it is not permitted to be laminated or composite in construction. The bowstave is cut from the radius of the tree so that sapwood (on the outside of the tree) becomes the back and forms about one third of the total thickness; the remaining two thirds or so is heartwood (50/50 is about the maximum sapwood/heartwood ratio generally used). Yew sapwood is good only in tension, while the heartwood is good in compression.

Flatbows

American flatbows are very similar in construction to a longbow, except that a wider variety of wood is possible because of the cross-section of the bow's limbs being rectangular rather than D-section. Unlike a longbow, there is a shelf where the arrow contacts the bow which doubles as an arrow rest.

Wood for a flatbow may be elm, maple, sycamore, hazel, and ash. The bow may be as long as a longbow, but can also be much shorter in some cases.

The majority of traditional Native American bows were flatbows, as its shape holds several advantages over a D-section bow.

OTHER TRADITIONAL BOWS

Asiatic Bows

I expect a significant rise in interest in Asiatic bows since its 2022 inclusion in Archery GB's competition rules.

Put simply, the bow is composite in construction, short, with a recurve top and bottom. Competition rules allow for modern materials such as fibreglass or traditional such as bamboo, wood, or horn. Arrows are allowed to be metal, wood, carbon, or composite.

There is no shelf on the bow, no sight, no button, and no stabilisation.

What's the biggest difference? The string hand. Instead of three fingers around the string, the thumb goes around the string and the index finger then hooks over the thumbnail to help the hold. A ring is generally worn around the thumb to protect it from the string on release, in similar fashion to a tab, but it is made from leather, wood, jade, plastic, horn, or metal.

Horsebows

I hesitate to mention here (but I can't resist!) that I recently had to explain to one interested young bystander at the range that a horsebow is for shooting *from* a horse, not *at* a horse.

A horsebow, as mentioned in the chapter on archery types, is a compact recurve bow so that it can be easily manoeuvred across a horse's neck or rump to shoot forwards, backwards, and sideways. They are also popular with some field archery adherents and (where legal) bow-hunting enthusiasts, being short so that they are less likely to get encumbered climbing through undergrowth. Being short, however, they tend to be very snappy and unforgiving. Like Asiatic bows, they are often shot with the thumb rather than the fingers around the string.

Japanese Yumi

Japanese bows are very different from other bows across the world in that they are significantly asymmetric in their length—the top limb is about twice as long as the lower part. They are also generally much longer than other bow types, often up to 7' long. Materials in their manufacture are generally bamboo, leather, and wood, although some modern bows are also made from synthetic materials, with either hemp strings or modern materials.

While it is not known how it developed, it is possible that the shape developed for use on horseback, so the bow could be swung over the horse's neck to shoot on the other side, or that the bow needed to be shot from a kneeling position.

A yumi bow made from traditional materials takes a great deal of care and attention to keep it in good condition. Left unattended, the yumi can warp out of shape and may eventually become unusable.

CHAPTER 4

EQUIPMENT

LEFT OR RIGHT?

At first glance, this may be an odd question. Most people know if they're right- or left-handed from an early age. Many children know from playing football or other sports at school whether they favour their left or right foot. But which eye is dominant? The majority of people favour right eye if they're right-handed, or the left if left-handed. Cross-dominance, however, is by no means an unusual phenomenon and, I suspect, a genetically-inherited trait.

You can easily check which eye is dominant. With two hands, make a small triangle between your thumbs as per the diagram.

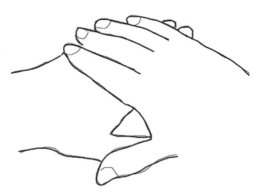

Looking through the small gap at a distant object, draw your hands back to your face, still looking at the far object. Whichever eye your hands come back to should be your dominant eye. Check this a couple of times.

Another method of checking your dominant eye is to point at a distant object with both eyes open and focussed on the object. Close one eye. If your finger now appears to be pointing at something else, you have just closed your dominant eye. Conversely, if you are still pointing at the object, your dominant eye is the one that remains open.

With strong eye dominance, you should shoot dependent on eye dominance, not hand dominance if there is a difference. So if you are left-handed but with right eye significantly dominant, you should shoot right-handed—in other words, your left hand will be your bow hand and your right hand will be your string or draw hand. However, if the dominance is not strong, some archers may be more comfortable shooting depending on hand dominance instead.

Much equipment is specific to left- or right-handed archers. This includes risers, sights, arrow rests, grips, tabs, quivers, and chest guards, so there is a lot to get wrong and a lot which needs to be specified when buying or selling.

WHAT EQUIPMENT WILL YOU NEED TO START?

Here is an initial list. You may get away with not getting every item on the list, but you'll be struggling. If you are unfamiliar with any terms, refer to the glossary at the back of the book.

➻ Bow, including riser, grip, limbs, string and nocking point, arrow rest, and sight (unless you're intending to shoot barebow) plus pressure button depending on arrow rest type
➻ Arrows
➻ Tab (finger guard), bracer (arm guard), quiver, bow stand, bag or case, stringer, and arrow puller

As you progress, you will want to add:

➻ Pressure button if not already in use
➻ Stabilisation, including long rod, side rods, V-bar, short extension, weights, dampers
➻ Clicker
➻ Basic tool kit (see the later chapter on maintenance for this)

Many archers, and especially women, will also need a chest protector that fits well.

Sourcing equipment can be time-consuming, particularly if your budget is limited. Often good deals can be had on eBay and elsewhere online such as Facebook Marketplace (but I strongly advise you to get the opinion of an experienced archer on any deals offered). Ensure also that you know exactly what is being offered— what is included when someone offers a bow for sale? The answer is that it can vary hugely. Aardvark Archery often have a good range of second-hand equipment, as do Clickers Archery, Wales Archery, Phoenix Archery, and Eagle Archery. It is well worth checking websites of suppliers in your area. There is a list of some retailers in the Links section at the end of the book.

BOW

If you skipped over the introduction to the book and my advice on buying or renting and what to buy or rent for what ages and stages of development, please go back and read it now.

As mentioned in the Introduction and chapter on archery types, there are several different disciplines within archery, all requiring different equipment. Indeed, there are quite a few Olympic recurve (or freestyle) archers who use different equipment for indoor and outdoor shooting. There are specialist barebow risers, but many barebow archers simply use a freestyle riser. If you are only just starting out on your archery adventure, I would not recommend buying anything specialist such as a barebow-specific riser, compound bow, or longbow.

The centre section of a recurve bow is called the riser. There are various different types. Most have detachable limbs for easy transport and storage and to allow changes to the limbs as your upper body fitness, strength, and technique improve or, in the case of juniors, simply as you grow. The majority of beginners' bows are generally called takedown bows. These often consist of a wooden (or sometimes metal or hard plastic) riser that is still capable of accepting mounting of more advanced sights, pressure buttons, arrow rests, and stabilisation. The limb generally attaches with a bolt placed through the limb and into the limb pocket on each end of the riser. See the colour illustrations.

The majority of Olympic recurve bows are what's called International Limb Fitting (ILF). The advantage of these risers is that there is a wide variety of manufacturers making limbs to the specification, in different draw weights, different materials (and thus different behaviour), and at widely varying prices.

There are some variations. Hoyt, an American manufacturer, as well as making ILF risers and limbs, also have their own specification called Formula. In these, the limb pockets are longer than ILF while being largely the same in all other respects. It was Hoyt who originally came up with the ILF specification, which they call Grand Prix. Note that an ILF limb will not fit a Formula riser, nor vice versa. Stylist Bows, a British manufacturer and renter of bows for anyone wanting to start out cheaply, have their own specification, and a Stylist riser has to have Stylist limbs. If you rent a bow from Stylist, you can swap limbs as many times as you like.

What Size Bow?

Put simply, work this out by measuring your arm span from fingertip to fingertip in inches, divide this figure by 2.5, which should approximate your draw length (of which more later), and add 40". Your bow should be no shorter than the resultant figure. Bows are almost always measured in inches, and include the riser and limbs. Limbs come in short, medium, and long varieties, which can be mixed with different risers to produce a wide variety of bow lengths, according to the following tables:

Bow Size Chart (Standard Limbs)			
Riser Length	Short Limbs	Medium Limbs	Long Limbs
Short Riser (23")	64" bow	66" bow	68" bow
Long Riser (25")	66" bow	68" bow	70" bow
X-Long Riser (27")	68" bow	70" bow	72" bow

Draw Length	Bow Length	
23" and under	62"	
23 to 25"	64"	Short riser and short limbs
25 to 27"	66"	Long riser and short limbs Short riser and medium limbs
27 to 30"	68"	Long riser and medium limbs Short riser and long limbs
30 to 32"	70"	Long riser and long limbs
31 to 34"	70-72"	X-Long riser and long limbs

If your calculated draw length comes out at, say, 24" then, looking at the second table, you will see that you would need a bow no less than 64" in total length. For anyone who has not yet finished growing, I would recommend considering a longer bow than that. A full-grown adult should not generally use a longer bow than required, simply for sake of the bow's efficiency. More on that below.

There are not many risers on the market at 27". Typically, a short riser with long limbs will be slower but more forgiving. A long riser with short limbs will be quite fast and snappy, but far less forgiving. The latter combination, unless you have a specific reason for needing it, should be avoided normally, as there is a danger at longer draw lengths of stacking the limbs (i.e., getting them to or past maximum designed bend and thus risking damage to them). There are some 21" risers around, but these are generally only used by field and 3D archers who need a shorter bow for climbing through undergrowth!

When choosing a riser, unless you think you won't grow out of the bow in a couple of years, I would suggest going for the most upmarket riser you can afford. A riser rarely wears out, and you should have it for many years.

As stated above, it would be a mistake to buy a recurve bow that is too long for you. If buying for a child who has not yet stopped growing, you might need to estimate the final draw length required, or simply buy shorter limbs. Why should you not buy or use a bow that is too long? Because it will be inefficient. The limbs of a recurve bow when drawn first flex, perhaps counter-intuitively, at the thickest area closest to the riser—the curve. Towards the end of full draw, the tips—the recurved sections— straighten out last and provide a significant part of the power of the bow. Thus a bow that is too long for the archer will not provide the best performance out of a shot (see the graph).

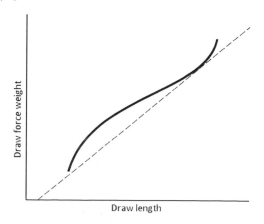

Draw length

As you can see from the graph, draw force weight is not linear. The bow only reaches peak efficiency once you reach the top end of the graph and draw force weight increases faster with increasing draw length.

Limbs

As mentioned above, there is a huge variety of limbs available for all sorts of bows. When you are starting out, you really do not want to spend a lot of money on a pair of limbs, which will last you probably only a year or three, depending on how much you shoot.

For an adult, I recommend no more than 22 lb limbs as a starter. I have seen so many new starters buy limbs of 28 lb, 34 lb, or even more, find that they are overbowed (i.e., they have a bow that needs too much power to draw) and have to change limbs again, or even get discouraged and give up the sport.

Children are more difficult to gauge for limbs. To start with, I would recommend absolutely no more than 16 lb limbs for any prepubescent child. Even in adolescence, bones are still growing and still soft, particularly at the ends at the joints. If a child is overbowed, they can do serious and permanent damage to their bones and future development. It is also easy to be deceived since, particularly with boys but also to a lesser extent with girls, strength develops before skeleton hardness and therefore the ability to pull a heavier draw bow is no guarantee that they should be doing so. A year or so after they have stopped growing is a safer time to increase the draw weight of their bow, which would normally not be until about age 18 or 19. Until then and post puberty, I would not let a child I'm coaching use a bow of more than 22 lbs, and then only if they have good shooting style.

String

If you buy a bow as a unit, you would expect to have a string supplied with it. This may not be the case, and you need to know how to buy a string. To start with, buy one off the shelf. You can often specify colours of string and servings, and you will need to specify what length bow the string is for. As the number of strands in a string will affect the speed of the bow and thus of the arrow, you may need to specify that detail as well. Given the variety of string materials available, my best advice is to consult the string maker, giving them your bow draw weight and your draw length. I would suggest that you buy a string that contrasts in colour with your riser and limbs to make it easier to see; see the section on string picture in the Technique chapter.

All string materials tend to a greater or lesser degree to stretch or creep. Note the difference between these two terms. *Stretch* means the string gets longer as tension is put into it by the bow being strung or drawn, and then returns to its former length when the tension is released. *Creep* is permanent; the string does not return to its former length at all. Most professional string makers will pre-creep a string before selling it. For an intermediate archer, some stretch is desirable—the string will be slightly more elastic and forgiving. A string with almost no stretch at all will be difficult for an inexperienced archer to handle. Therefore some stretch is desirable, creep less so. As a string creeps you will need to continue to put more and more twists in it to keep the effective string length consistent.

Nocking Point

If you have bought a new string, you will need to set up your nocking point. Some archers use thread glued in place. Don't do anything that will make it too permanent until you are happy with the tuning of the whole system. Brass nocks are a good temporary solution, but in the long run will tear a strip into the leather of your tab. They also have the effect of slowing the string down, which will be covered in the section on bow tuning.

Where to set your nocking point? Here's where you will need to buy or borrow a brace height gauge. It clips on the string and shows you both brace height (as its name suggests!) and how high above the arrow rest you could place the nocking point. The best starting point is to place the bottom nocking point such that the arrow nock is 5mm (about 1/5") above the arrow rest, so slightly tilted downwards toward the point. When it comes to tuning, this may well need to be adjusted. In the past the recommendation was about 3mm, but thinking on this has changed.

Sight

Here again there are great differences to be had. If you are intending to stick with barebow, of course, you won't need a sight at all. Otherwise, an inexpensive sight will cost you around £20. It does the same job as a sight that costs £400, so what's the difference? Put simply, adjustability. A cheap sight will be less easily adjustable, less solid, with screws which can come loose with vibration of the bow. I have lost count of the number of times I've seen archers confused that their shots are suddenly going high on the target, only to realise later that their sight is gradually slipping down the rail, or others who have found that the sight just drops off the bow. Yes, you can do the screws up tighter—so tight that you have difficulty undoing them when you want to adjust—but no matter how tight you do them, sooner or later they will work loose, and you'll find that you need to check the tightness of everything every time you come to the shooting line. If you can afford it, I would recommend spending no less than around £100 on a sight at current (2022) prices. Like the riser, it will last you for a long time and cause much less irritation than a cheap sight.

Most sight rings are circular, which can easily be visually placed around the gold of the target; some have a square outer section, which assists in seeing if you are canting the bow to either side. Personal preference comes into play here. Some sight pins are solid; some are coloured fibre which shows up as a bright spot in the middle of your sight. Generally sight pins are interchangeable.

Arrow Rest

Arrow rests, like almost everything else, come in cheap and cheerful versions and horrendously expensive designs that will cost you a lot more. The Koreans, who are always the nation to beat at the Olympics, use simple plastic arrow rests which cost about £2 each. These simple rests have a built-in pressure point for the arrow to rest against and push against on its way from the bow as you shoot. Problems include the plastic softening over time and needing frequent replacement. They are also impossible to adjust.

More sophisticated rests need a pressure button to provide the pressure point for the arrow. This allows you to adjust the arrow to the centre of the bow and to adjust the spring-loaded plunger to absorb some of the bend in the arrow as it leaves the bow.

Mid-range rests, like the plastic ones, also stick on the riser with a double-sided sticky pad. If you put them in the wrong place you will then find that removing them is difficult, as is cleaning off the excess sticky stuff. If you go for one of these, make sure you keep a spare sticky pad or two in your bow bag, as sooner or later you will find your rest dropping off, as I once found when I had no spare with me and had to sacrifice an evening's shooting. A wrap-around rest which bolts onto the riser is basically inexpensive and easier (well, actually less difficult) to adjust. If you have bought a wooden takedown bow then your options are going to be a bit more limited.

Button (or Plunger)

If you've gone for a cheap plastic arrow rest, you won't need a button at all. And even if the rest is more up-market, for a button you can quite safely take the inexpensive route to start. Once you have set it up and tuned your bow, you shouldn't need to adjust the button at all unless you change arrows, and then you're into retuning the whole system anyway. If you combine a button with the plastic type of arrow rest, there is a small tab on the rest close to the hole for the button which you will need to cut off as with a button this tab is superfluous.

The button is the second point after the arrow rest on which the arrow touches the bow. It is designed firstly to adjust the lateral position of the arrow on the bow and also how much of the bend of the arrow is absorbed and damped out as it leaves the bow.

Archers who regularly shoot different sets of arrows (this is not uncommon with barebow archers) will need either a button that is easily adjustable to predetermined settings or a set of buttons that can easily be swapped out of the riser and replaced with another with different settings of the internal spring and plunger.

Clicker

Also called a draw check indicator. Barebow archers are not allowed to compete with a clicker on the bow. I recommend, however, that they have one available in their bag for training purposes to find and get used to the feel of where full draw is for them.

You won't need this until your draw length has settled down (it will increase as you practise and improve your technique) and you can then have a set of arrows cut to the right length for your draw length and bow set-up. However, there is nothing wrong with buying one when getting the rest of your gear as it can sit on the riser unused until you are ready, but if you do, make sure it is one of the cheaper versions.

What does it do? Put simply, it helps you ensure that your draw length is consistent from one arrow to the next. If you were to draw an arrow further than the previous one, this one will go higher up the target than the previous one. Conversely, an arrow drawn short will hit the target lower down. So, as you draw, with the blade of the clicker resting on the outer edge of the arrow, you aim at full draw, then expand (see the chapter on technique) and partway through expansion, the clicker blade meets the tip of the arrow and falls back past it, making an audible click. You have, of course, been expecting this and are holding your aim as you gradually expand, and you then release immediately on the clicker sound. Thus your draw length is the same every arrow.

I generally recommend that people place a little blob of something easily visible such as white paint (I use correcting fluid) just behind where the clicker blade comes against the clicker plate so it's easy to tell with a glance each time if the clicker has moved. And believe me, almost all cheaper clickers will move.

Grip

The grip of the riser on all but the least expensive takedown bows is removable and replaceable. The easiest variable to change is the angle between the part against which the palm of your hand fits and the vertical. This will depend on personal choice, individual anatomy, and, to a certain extent, age and flexibility. Some archers with access to the right equipment (or good friends!) have custom-made grips 3D printed for them in their choice of colour. Others make their own wooden grips, sanding them down or building them up with wood filler, plaster, or tape layers.

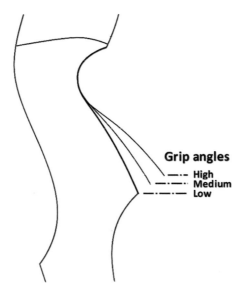

Grip angles
—··— High
—·—·· Medium
—·—·— Low

If you are just starting out on the path of buying your own equipment, try different risers, and, if available, different grips until you find one that is comfortable. Then go with that.

Stabilisation

Stabilisers, dampers, long rods, side rods, V-bars, and short extensions will not be needed until your coach has seen that your bow hand is consistent and you are not gripping the bow at any point during the shot sequence. One coach of my acquaintance has been known to go along a shooting line and say to archers "Can I have your stabiliser?" When asked why, his response is "Because you're not using it with your death grip like that!" Getting the bow hand right can take a while.

The purpose of stabilisation is held in a clue in the name. It improves mostly lateral stability of the bow by having a very light carbon rod hold a weight out in front of the bow whose inertia thus inhibits some of its lateral movement. As that weighs down the bow away from the archer, generally people also have a couple of weights behind the long rod on V-bars which counterbalance part of the down force. The back weights very often will be of unequal masses to counteract the weight of the sight and button on the far side of the riser. All these weights should have rubber dampers between them and the carbon rods to absorb vibration.

ARROWS

There is a huge amount that can be (and already has been) written about arrows, including choice, variety, expense, and personal taste therein.

Arrows vary in length, spine stiffness (both static and dynamic), pile (or point) shape and weight, nock type, fletching materials, size, and shape. I won't go into the method of defining arrow spine, diameter, wall thickness etc. here because different manufacturers use different coding methods.

For a starting arrow, go for something inexpensive; you're going to need to change it before too long. It will need to be more or less matched to your bow, draw weight, and draw length. A set of twelve inexpensive aluminium arrows should cost in the region of £70–80. Normally you will shoot six arrows per end on an outdoor range. You will also need spares quickly to hand—arrows can quite easily get lost, damaged, or broken. For tuning the system you will also need at least one arrow that has no fletchings.

To decide what spine and type of arrows you need, download the latest Easton Arrow chart from their website, and you can either use the app on the website or print out the chart itself and check your details on there. A brief description follows, but for detailed instructions on how to use the chart, I strongly suggest you get a coach or other experienced archer to show you.

Your Arrow			Length for Target · Field · 3D						Recurve bow
24"	25"	26"	27"	28"	29"	30"	31"	32"	Bow weight in lb.
01	02	03	T1	T2	T3				21–27 lb. (9.5–12.2 kg)
02	03	T1	T2	T3	T4	T5			27–32 lb. (12.2–14.5 kg)
03	T1	T2	T3	T4	T5	T6	T7		32–36 lb. (14.5–16.3 kg)
T1	T2	T3	T4	T5	T6	T7	T8	T9	36–40 lb. (16.3–18.1 kg)
T2	T3	T4	T5	T6	T7	T8	T9	T10	40–44 lb. (18.1–20.0 kg)
T3	T4	T5	T6	T7	T8	T9	T10	T11	44–48 lb. (20.1–21.8 kg)
T4	T5	T6	T7	T8	T9	T10	T11	T12	48–52 lb. (21.8–23.6 kg)
T5	T6	T7	T8	T9	T10	T11	T12	T13	53–57 lb. (24.0–25.9 kg)
T6	T7	T8	T9	T10	T11	T12	T13	T13	58–62 lb. (26.3–28.1 kg)
T7	T8	T9	T10	T11	T12	T13	T13	T14	63–67 lb. (28.6–30.4 kg)
T8	T9	T10	T11	T12	T13	T13	T14		68–73 lb. (30.8–33.1 kg)

Find your draw length and bow draw weight in the table. For barebow archers, instead of draw length, use desired arrow length—this will depend to a certain extent on the distances at which you want to shoot. For a recurve bow up to 27 lbs and a draw length of 29", you will see that the recommended arrow group is T3.

Group T3			
*720–280 R	0.720–0.780	A/C/E	6.4
*700–750 R	0.700–0.750	X10	6.7
720	0.720	ProTour	6.2
*710–810 R	0.710–0.810	A/C/G	6.5
3X–04	0.830	A/C/C	6.7
3L–04	0.750	A/C/C	7.0
730	0.730	Carb1	6.0
750	0.750	Inspire	8.1
840	0.840	Apollo	6.5
1813	0.874	75	7.9
1814	0.799	X7	8.6
1816	0.756	75	9.3

Key	
A/C/C	Aluminum/Carbon/Composite
A/C/E	Aluminum/Carbon/Extreme
A/C/G	A/C/G (Aluminum/Carbon)
Apollo	Apollo
Carb1	Carbon One
FMJMatch	FMJ Match
HSpeed	Hyperspeed
Inspire	Inspire
Pro	ProComp
ProTour	X10 ProTour Shafts (Aluminum/Carbon)
SDRIVE 27	Super Drive 27
SDRIVE 25	Super Drive 25
SDRIVE 23	Super Drive 23
X7	X7 Eclipse (7178-T9 alloy)
X10	X10 Shafts (Aluminum/Carbon)
75	XX75: Platinum Plus, Tribute, Jazz and Neos (7075 alloy)
RX7	RX7 Tapered (7178-T9 alloy)

*When two sizes are listed together, the weight listed is for the first shaft.

Now drop down to the relevant group (T3 for this example) and you will see the above sub-table (left). This shows the size, spine, model, and weight in grains/inch of arrows recommended for your bow's draw weight and your draw length.

If you are going for the cheap and cheerful option here (see 75 in the key on the right), then XX75, Platinum Plus, Tribute, Jazz, and Neos arrows are the ones for you, and you will need to order arrows with 1813 or 1816 spine. The difference between those two is on the second page (not shown) where the stiffness of the two spines is shown—the 1813s are weaker spined.

If you want more expensive arrows, ACGs might suit you in 810 spine, and you will then have further decisions to make about piles (points) and nock types.

Please don't be tempted to cut arrows down to your draw length until your form has stabilised. Even then, cutting arrows is a specialist job and needs experience—don't take a hacksaw to your arrows! Any reputable retailer will do this for you.

Fibreglass Arrows

Avoid. There is generally a maximum draw weight these can be used with, and you don't want to forget that and shatter a fibreglass arrow close to your face.

Aluminium Arrows

These are very popular with beginners and early intermediate archers. They are inexpensive and relatively hard-wearing. Many clubs use these on beginner's courses so the chances are that you will have met them. If they get slightly bent, it is possible to straighten them but the results are only ever approximate, and it is easier to bin them. If they get lost in the grass, they are generally very easy to find using a metal detector.

Aluminium/Carbon Composite Arrows

These are a very good, generally mid-priced choice for the slightly more advanced intermediate archer. Composite arrows combine lightness with remarkable strength. Easton used to make an arrow called ACC, but have now discontinued it, which I felt at the time was a pity as they were very popular in the UK at least, and many archers used them even at competition standard. ACC are still available from most retailers, but there are signs that stocks are starting to diminish at time of writing. There are substitutes, however. Some arrows (e.g., Easton's ACEs) are not cylindrical but slightly barrel-shaped along their length and so require care in cutting all arrows of a set in exactly the same way.

Carbon Arrows

Care is needed with all-carbon arrows. If shot into a straw target boss, they can get damaged fairly easily. They are harder to find with a metal detector (some people put a thin section of aluminium kitchen foil inside the arrow for this purpose) and some clubs forbid their use altogether, particularly if the range is not 24/7 and animals graze there. A broken carbon arrow can have very thin shards which get under the skin and cause serious irritation. They can also cause havoc with a grass cutter!

All that said, carbon arrows have very good performance, don't bend, and are very popular with top-notch archers. They can also be very expensive!

Spine

As mentioned above, arrows are measured by spine static and dynamic stiffness. Static spine can be easily measured by placing the arrow horizontally on a pair of rests and hanging a weight from the middle. The amount the centre of the arrow bends is its declared spine, and this information is included on the shaft of the arrow. It is static spine stiffness which will dictate what arrow is best for your draw length and bow draw weight.

Dynamic spine is a slightly more difficult concept and can be adjusted. Put simply, this is how an arrow actually behaves in flight, so cannot be measured. It can, however, be adjusted by changing the speed of the string, the power of the bow, the type and size of fletches, the weight of the arrow pile, and even the type of nocking point indicator. More of this in the section on tuning.

Fletches

What shape, material, size? First off, for anything other than traditional and longbow shooting, NOT feathers. They look great, but are expensive, don't like getting wet, and are prone to damage. At your stage of shooting, I also recommend keeping away from spin vanes.

For a first set of arrows, I'd suggest simple plastic vanes. They're very inexpensive, come in all sorts of sizes, shapes, and colours, and are easily replaced if they get damaged or lost.

There is a fairly simple art to fletching arrows, and I suggest you watch and learn from someone else before attempting the deed yourself, for which you will need to buy or borrow a fletching jig.

As far as size goes, the larger the vane, the more stable laterally and the slower the arrow BUT the more susceptible to cross-winds. Because of Archer's Paradox (see the chapter on bow types), a small vane takes a while to straighten an arrow in flight. Hence indoors, where flight distance is at a premium and cross-winds are not a problem, archers use large fletches. Outside, particularly over longer distances, small fletches, which slow the arrow less and are less susceptible to cross-winds are more popular. For the speeds of lighter draw weight bows, by which I mean less than about 18 lbs, I'd suggest 1.6" vanes. AAE Plastifletch vanes are graded by size—EP16s are just over 1.6" long, EP23s just over 2.3" long, and so on. Other manufacturers have different product references.

Piles

No, not a nasty affliction, but the technical name for the pointy bit of an arrow—the end intended to hurt. Once again, to start with go for whatever the basic arrow comes with. Take advice from the shop.

With your next set of arrows and as you progress, you can be a bit more adventurous. Different weight piles will affect the tuning of the whole system since a heavier weight pile will slow down the front of the arrow as it comes off the bow while the impetus comes at the back of the arrow, thus increasing the bend in the shaft. This is dynamic spine weakening, as you will have learned from the section above on arrow spine. A lighter pile will cause the arrow to act as if its spine were stiffer. Put simply, a light draw weight will need a weak-spined arrow. Heavier bows require stiffer arrows for best performance and tuning.

Some piles are screwed into inserts within the arrow. These therefore can be removed easily and swapped or replaced. The majority of piles are glued in using a type of glue that softens with heat application and therefore needs a source of strong heat such as a small blowtorch to fix or remove the piles.

Some piles are sold with break-off shafts. You can therefore make each pile lighter simply by taking a hacksaw or stout pair of pliers to the shaft of the pile itself.

TAB

The purpose of a finger tab is twofold. Firstly, it will protect the fingers of your draw hand from the string as you pull and on release. It also provides a smooth surface so that the string can slide easily when you relax the fingers. Another point of a tab is to assist in providing good anchoring and reference of the draw to the same point on your face every shot, thus aiding consistency.

There are, once again, several types. Specialist tabs for barebow archers usually have no slot in the middle, although some do as barebow archers sometimes need to shoot split-finger (i.e., with one finger above the arrow on the string and two fingers below). The most straightforward tab is simply a piece of shaped leather with a couple of holes strategically placed for fingers. These should cost no more than a couple of pounds in the UK. From there we go steadily more and more expensive. The most expensive have great adjustability for different shape hands with brass backing plates, and can cost anything up to £70.

For a relatively new archer, almost anything will do for the first few outings to the range. See what other archers use, and ask them what they like or dislike about particular types. Thereafter, take a trip to your nearest supplier and try different types. I would recommend one with a finger spacer or intermediate shelf but without a top shelf as it can interfere with getting to a consistent anchor point.

These all come in different sizes, so it is worth knowing what size you need before ordering and, of course, are specific to left- or right-handed. To the best of my knowledge, none are ambidextrous.

BRACER OR ARM GUARD

Whichever name you use for it, a bracer is a particularly useful and important item for a new archer. It straps to your bow arm to protect the forearm from the string as you release. A secondary purpose is keeping bulkier clothing away from the string.

Some have fastenings with hooks and eyes on elastic straps, some velcro, some push clips, and Bohning make one that pulls over your whole forearm like an elastic sleeve.

If, like some, your elbow is prone to over-extension, I would recommend the type of bracer which extends above the elbow. This type is also quite good for youngsters whose tendency to grip the bow brings their forearm close to the string. The smallest and lightest, which are little more than a strip of plastic with a couple of straps attached, I would not recommend to beginners or lower-intermediate archers.

CHEST GUARD

A large percentage of women—and quite a few men as well—will benefit from wearing a chest guard. Chest guards will keep clothing out of the way and help avoid snagging. Different clothing can easily alter the travel of the bowstring as you release and thus affect results at the target. Therefore the chest guard will also give a consistent surface for the string to sit against, whatever your clothing on the day. The most obvious benefit, of course, is avoiding a nipple being snagged under light clothing by the string as you release, which can certainly bring tears to the eyes. It is well worthwhile spending some time trying different sizes and designs to find the best fit.

QUIVER

You will need one. For a few outings you can get by without, but putting arrows on the ground really isn't an option. Ground quivers are available for outdoor ranges, which are a spike driven into the ground with a ring and hooks at the top for the arrows and bow when not shooting. Ground quivers for indoor use are very expensive. So buy yourself a quiver.

Look at what others are using. Once again, ask questions. Prices can vary hugely, and bear in mind that there is a version of Parkinson's Law which applies to quivers and archery bags, in that the number and total size of the items to be stored expand as the size of the container increases. Pockets for tabs, score cards, mobile phone, small towel, or tassel, clips and loops will all be useful. Most are sold with plastic tubes to keep arrows from bunching together too much and thus damaging fletches. Some have two tubes, most have three or more. I would advise against a quiver with only two tubes. I would also advise against the type that come without a belt, and simply have a clip to hang on your own waistband or belt. These can be extremely annoying, particularly if your waistband is not immediately available under clothing. If you don't happen to be wearing a belt, they can also make you uncomfortable with pulling at your waistband. Being uncomfortable while shooting will not help your performance!

BOW STAND

There's not a lot to say about bow stands. You will need to put your bow down somewhere when you go downrange to collect your arrows from the target or are simply taking a break, and putting a bow on the ground is not a good idea. On your beginner's course the club may have provided a rack into which everyone could place their bows, but these are generally only available during a course.

Most bow stands break down and fold up easily for storage. Some simply fold up, while with others the legs detach on magnets and are placed in alternate holes in the base parallel to the upright. Quite a few have a clip on the upright for the string when the riser is placed in the cradle at the top. These clips do help keep the bow from tipping the ends of one limb or the other into the mud! A cradle which actually holds the grip of the riser is infinitely to be preferred in my opinion to a simple U-shaped solid cradle.

My preferred stand has a swing-out arm which takes the long rod stabiliser and holds the bow at an angle, which is a great help when adjusting the button plunger or arrow rest without the immediate benefit of a bow vice.

And beware! Quite a few bow stands have an integrated ground spike to hold the stand when outside—if yours has one of these, ensure it is removed or retracted before using it indoors, particularly with a nice wooden floor!

BAG OR CASE

At its simplest, a bow bag will hold an unstrung and disassembled bow, a sight, a stringer, a few spares, and a set of arrows, all nicely scrunched up and ready to get damaged, broken, or bent.

Either buy a bag with an integrated arrow tube, or get yourself a separate arrow tube for storage and transport. An alternative to an arrow tube is to repurpose a poster or carpet cardboard tube.

Note that bags and cases for compound bows are very different, since they need to hold the bow fully strung as you very, very rarely unstring a compound bow.

As I've said above, Parkinson's Law applies to bow bags, and, no matter the size of it, you will always be running out of space. So buy a big one. Most archers of my acquaintance use bags equipped with wheels or straps so it can be pulled behind or carried on the back, since a full bow bag can get heavy. Lots of extra zipped pockets inside or out will always be useful.

STRINGER

If you're getting into compound archery, you won't need one. For all other bows, there are two ways to string a bow—the wrong way and with a stringer. I won't go into the wrong way here—this book is intended to keep you out of bad habits, not to teach you how to get into them!

There aren't many types of stringers out there. Some are simply a cord with a leather loop (for the top limb) on one end and a leather pocket (for the bottom limb) on the other. In my experience, this type can get tangled easily in your bag, but they are easily adjustable to your bow length and your arm reach, by the simple measure of putting a few knots in the cord. The other type—which I prefer—is a length of broad, tough nylon ribbon, once again with pocket and loop on either end. Longbow archers should use a tip-to-tip stringer, which has pockets on both ends.

See the chapter on technique for using a stringer.

BOW SLING

To start with, using a light draw bow and with beginner's form and no stabilisation on the bow, you won't need a sling. It is, however, something that shortly will become indispensable. Which type is strongly a matter of personal taste, so be prepared to buy and try a variety. None are particularly expensive, so this shouldn't be financially burdensome!

The purpose of a sling is to stop the bow springing out of your hand and landing face down in the mud much to the amusement of archers around you at your expense. As a coach, I love seeing this, as it will only happen when your bow hand form is correct (and, later on, you have forgotten to do up your sling).

Finger slings are, in effect, a shoelace tied in a loop. One end goes around your thumb. The whole thing loops round the back of the bow grip onto your index or middle finger.

Wrist slings go around your wrist with an extra loop to go around the bow grip and then clip back into the sling itself.

Bow slings attach to the back of the bow and you simply slip your hand through when you pick the bow up, with no need to unclip or untie anything. Without a stabiliser long rod, you will need a keeper bolt to hold one of this type in place in use.

Buckle slings are the one type I will caution you NOT to buy. They attach too low on the bow, and do not allow you to control the bow through the follow-through stage of the shot.

Slings are one of many areas where you will benefit greatly from talking to other archers, seeing what they use, and possibly, if they are feeling generous, being able to borrow theirs to try out.

ARROW PULLER

Once again, there are lots out there. An arrow puller is basically a lump of rubber with a groove down the middle so that it folds around the shaft of an arrow to provide better grip to pull it out of the boss (or wood of the target stand!). Some work, some don't. You will need one, so once again, see what other archers recommend.

EQUIPMENT OPTIONS

For some, getting fully kitted-out will be a significant struggle financially, but going into an archery supplies shop and selecting the nasal payment option is not your only possible course.

Buying New

If you find that a hitherto unknown aunt has left you lots of money in her will, then by all means buy new. But even then I'm sure you wouldn't want to waste money. Bear in mind that as you progress (and here I'm assuming that you are just starting out on your archery career) your form will improve, your upper body fitness will get better, your strength and draw length will increase.

Bear in mind also that it is well worthwhile looking at the websites of suppliers and comparing prices.

Buy the best riser you can afford. Initially buy inexpensive limbs—you will need to replace them fairly soon. Get a halfway decent sight, and a good quiver. Buy a bracer that is comfortable and fits well, and a tab that behaves similarly. Get a bag that is more than big enough for everything on your shopping list. Almost everything else you will gradually replace anyway as each item wears out.

Buy inexpensive arrows—at the beginning is when you are most likely to lose or damage arrows, and you will want better arrows sooner or later anyway, so there is little point in spending a fortune on them now.

Buying Second-Hand

There is a large marketplace out there in second-hand archery equipment. Various web-based markets such as eBay, Facebook Marketplace, and several Facebook groups exist since people tire of archery, have deceased relatives' kit to sell, or want to upgrade. As I mentioned at the start of this chapter, several suppliers offer second-hand equipment for sale, and there is a list in the Links section of this book.

If you go via the second-hand route, do not be in such a hurry to buy that you don't get full details of what's on offer. Get all the specifications you can, and show them to experienced archers or a coach in your club and get their opinion and advice. Be aware also that there is a flourishing market in stolen archery equipment so if a seller appears not to know much about the equipment or is evasive when asked questions, be on your guard.

Don't be tempted to overbow yourself—to use limbs that are too heavy for you. As I've said elsewhere in this book, just after completing a beginner's course I would recommend no more than 22lb limbs even for a grown man.

When buying second-hand arrows, be very sure that they are long enough for you. Arrows that are too long are not a safety issue. Arrows that are too short are very dangerous. You will need arrows which are about 2" longer than your draw length.

Renting

Some clubs offer rental options to new members, and, where available, this is well worth considering.

The only equipment suppliers that I know of which offers rental services are Stylist Bows and Urban Archers, whom I mentioned at the start of this chapter. They will allow you to swap limbs as many times as you need, and, if you like and want to keep the bow, will discount the rental already paid from the purchase price. The only problem thereafter with renting a Stylist bow would be that you can only use Stylist limbs on a Stylist riser.

Renting a bow in the early years of your archery career is quite a good option which can keep your costs low. After a year or two you will have a much better idea of what you like, what sort of archery you prefer, and therefore what kit will best suit you.

CHAPTER 5

ANATOMY

Some understanding of basic anatomy and physiology is helpful in knowing how to achieve and maintain good form in an archer. It is highly desirable to cultivate an awareness of which muscles are doing what at any particular moment, and similar awareness of how the skeleton is aligned and thus whether it is bone or brawn which is holding your bow steady.

This chapter is not intended as a complete source of reference in the subject of human anatomy and development, and there are several excellent books available for further reading if desired. See the Further Reading section at the end of the book for references.

The intention of an archer is to be able to use the system—the archer's body, accessories such as tab, the bow itself, and arrows—to hit as close to the point of aim as possible as often as possible and to be able to keep this up for as long as required. I insert a reminder at this point that some competition formats can last several hours. Stamina is therefore as important as strength and form.

You will want to transfer power from your body into bending the limbs of the bow as effectively as possible, and then in a further transfer from the bow to the arrow to propel it as efficiently as possible, and preferably in the direction you require!

First, therefore a good, stable basis is required in feet, legs, and core. Second, good power is needed to transfer as much energy as possible into the arrow, and third, good confirmation is needed in feedback, not only visually in seeing where the arrow struck the target, but mainly through feeling how a shot went. With just a little practice you will very quickly learn how to recognise where you went wrong on a shot and what is needed to correct it on the next shot. This is not, however, to be taken as a replacement for observation and feedback from a good coach. It is very easy to slip into bad habits in archery without being aware of them, and critical feedback will almost always be useful.

It should be clear that muscles tire in prolonged use or under excessive demand. Keeping a limb still using muscles alone by balancing pairs of opposing muscles is going to tire them and contribute to unintentional input to either the bow hand, draw hand, or other areas of the body. The aim, therefore, should be to use as few muscles as little as possible in order to be able to keep up optimum performance as long as possible.

Any understanding of mechanics will show that a force applied along a straight line of incompressible, inflexible material will not move it, that a triangle is a rigid structure, and therefore using the best properties of the skeleton will help you to use muscles as little as possible in raising, drawing, and aiming a bow.

SKELETON

It should be fairly obvious that the skeleton is basically a hard frame on which the rest of the human body is attached. This hard frame, however, has weaknesses, is still soft until growth has stopped, and, in some individuals, has entirely missing elements.

I am not going to go into detail of every bone in the human body, all 206 of them. From the feet up, however, the legs, pelvis, and spine I shall treat for the purposes of this book as simply the (hopefully) stable base for the rest of the archer—shoulders, arms, neck, head, and hands.

ACHIEVING STRAIGHT LINES

Seen from the archer's three o'clock position, feet are about the same distance apart as shoulders, upright, and thus with all elements of the skeleton in alignment. See the top figure on the following page.

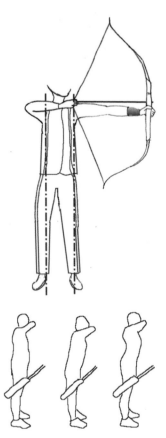

From the archer's six o'clock position, the left image shows a good, upright stance. The middle shows leaning forward, which would require muscle use to hold, and the right shows an arched back, the spine bent, and thus also requiring muscle usage.

Note that a normal stance gives us a curved spine, and we actually want to avoid that here while we twist towards the target. Therefore, it is necessary to adopt a stance which initially will feel very strange, unfamiliar, and unnatural. To achieve that, the easiest way to describe it is a slump as if you are about to sit down. This will rotate the pelvis forward—note, do not push it forward—and thus move the base of the spine backwards, straightening the normal curve. You can check this yourself by using a long mirror at home, with a piece of masking tape placed vertically to judge the curve or otherwise of your spine. This vertical line can also help you judge when using an exercise band whether you are committing the sin of leaning backwards as you draw.

The figures on the right show alignment as seen from above. The top figure shows good alignment from bow hand to elbow to shoulder to opposite shoulder in a straight line. Meanwhile, there is another straight line from arrow point to draw hand to draw elbow. These two lines make a tight, narrow triangle with the upper part of the draw arm. The second figure shows the same as the first but simplified.

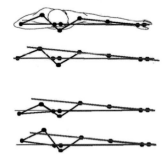

In the third figure, the archer's elbow is forward, as is the shoulder of the draw arm. You can see how this affects stability and would use muscle strength to keep steady as opposed to using the rigidity of the skeleton frame in the first figure. A similar problem arises in the bottom figure, where the elbow has been pulled too far back in a fit of overenthusiasm.

As the quick and enquiring mind will infer from the figure above, the only place in which the entire arm and shoulder joins to the rest of the skeleton is via the clavicle (or collar bone) onto the sternum (breast bone). An archer particularly needs to understand the difference between rotating the arm at the shoulder and movement of the whole shoulder. This latter movement is that achieved by imagining trying to pinch a finger between your shoulder blades. An alternative is to hold your forearm horizontal in front of your face with your elbow bent at ninety degrees and, without changing the angle of the elbow, bring your forearm in towards your face. This is the sort of movement required in the expansion phase of the shot cycle—see the chapter on technique for more on this.

BOW HAND POSITIONING

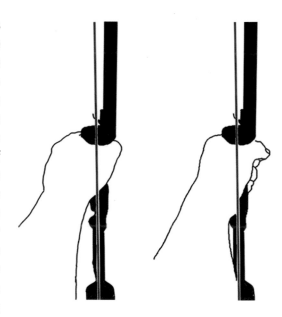

In the chapter on technique is a description of how to get the perfect hand position on the bow. This is important for two reasons. First, if you feel at the base of your thumb, there is a bone which is where the bones of the hand join the bones of the wrist. That is therefore the first point of contact of the bow to the (hopefully) rigid structure up one arm and across your shoulders with a slight angle down to the elbow of your draw arm. If all those are as close to a straight line as possible, holding a bow at full draw will be far less tiring than otherwise since all the compression is on a solid, straight line. Second, with your bow hand in the correct position, your forearm will be kept away from the string—and that is desirable because otherwise the shot will go adrift from where you intended and also you will find it painful!

Thus, if any archer complains to me that the string is catching their forearm or their bracer, my first instinct is to check their bow hand and ensure they are not gripping the bow. This can be slightly more difficult for someone whose elbow naturally overextends (i.e., appears to bend backwards).

SKELETON STRUCTURE

Bones are not solid. They are actually a honeycomb structure with a hollow centre which contains the bone marrow, which produces red blood cells, white blood cells, and platelets.

Bones link together at joints, the majority of which are synovial joints. Holding bone to bone is the function of ligaments, and linking muscles to bones is the job of tendons. Damaging either tendons or ligaments can be painful, and while a damaged tendon will put you out of action for a while, repairing ligaments is lengthy and difficult. Osteoarthritis can occur when overusing a joint or mistreating it, particularly after an operation or injury. Archery is a significantly asymmetric sport and thus the risk of injury is high unless care is taken.

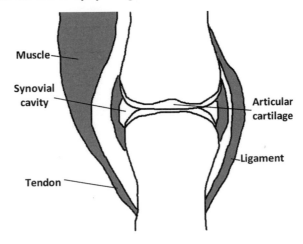

In this simplified diagram, the basic structure of a synovial joint can be seen. While joints such as this have good performance under compression, tension is not so good, nor is impact. Synovial fluid acts as both lubricant and cushion.

The shoulder is a ball-and-socket joint, as is the hip. However, the shoulder has only a very shallow socket which can thus give very wide range of movement, but which is capable of damage without sufficient care. To facilitate this wide range of movement there are a variety of muscles acting at the shoulder, of which more later. As stated earlier, the only direct mechanical connection between the arm and the rest of the skeleton is via the clavicle where it joins to the sternum, a joint which has very limited range of movement. Furthermore, the only thing stopping completely free movement of the shoulder blade and associated joints is attached muscle.

MUSCLES

The muscles which are most important in an archer are those of the back, neck, and arms. While I will name them you don't need to remember all of them, but you do need to be able to identify which you are using at any particular time and for particular movements or for maintaining position and posture.

Not all the muscles of the human body are under your conscious control, of course, just skeletal muscles and a few others. Consider the muscles of the heart and digestive system and you will realise you have no control over them whatsoever. Other muscles are only partially under conscious control and act without thinking about, such as the mechanism for breathing or blinking.

The chemical changes that occur in muscles to enable them to work are outside the scope of this book, but put briefly, an oversimplification is that oxygen in the blood is used as fuel, and the by-products of the reaction such as lactic acid need to be removed.

The more muscles are used, the more likely you are to tire quickly, and the more likely to be unable to keep steady as you aim. For this reason, your stance needs to be neutral—your feet a shoulder width apart, knees straight but not locked, and as you come to full aim, your bow arm should be straight but not locked, and your head turned towards the target and held still, but not turned so much that it is pulled back as you draw.

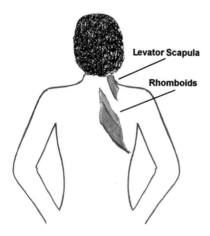

Deeper muscles of the back.

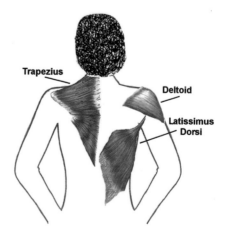

Upper muscles of the back.

You use muscles in your neck (splenial, sternocleidomastoid, and levator scapula) to move your head and keep it steady. The deltoid muscle in the shoulder is responsible for raising the bow. The muscle responsible for keeping the shoulder down and thus helping to a significant degree in the draw is called the latissimus dorsi, and is situated below the shoulder blade and attached to the spine. This is a large muscle, and therefore will tire less easily than smaller muscles trying to do the same job. The other muscles involved in the draw are the trapezius, which is in effect three muscles all on its own, upper, middle, and lower, plus the rhomboids major and minor and the subscapularis, one of the muscles to stabilise the rotator cuff of the shoulder which thus acts as a powerful defence to the front of the shoulder joint, preventing displacement of the head of the humerus (bone of the upper arm).

The trapezius is a large muscle, extending from the spine right at the top of the neck down to mid-back and outwards to the top of the scapula. This is a useful muscle for an archer! It is the upper trapezius which will tend to pull your head away from the target as you draw if you have turned your head too far—see chapter 6 on technique.

The rhomboids pull the scapula towards the spine. They don't extend above the shoulder line, nor below the scapula. They therefore come into use during expansion.

Latissimus dorsi is another big muscle. It is a broad sheet of muscle, extending from the outer shoulder directly across to the spine, from a point adjacent to the scapula, down the spine as far as the pelvis. It will keep your shoulders down as you raise the bow and draw it and is therefore a big help in drawing. Allowing your shoulder to lift as you raise the bow will keep this useful muscle inactive and therefore tire you more quickly.

If you draw using the wrong muscles, once you get to full draw and your muscles are under strain, it is effectively impossible to transfer the load to the correct muscles (latissimus dorsi, rhomboids, and trapezius). Keeping your shoulder down as you raise the bow and before you draw is therefore vitally important to your stamina and to the steadiness of your shot. This is also partly why it is important not to draw as you raise the bow but to keep the two movements separate.

Clearly you will be using muscles in your forearm. Located here are the wrist flexors and extensors. Don't use them! If you draw the string straight back towards your face, you will cock your wrist and use muscles you don't have to. The draw should come from the elbow of your draw arm, keeping a straight line from elbow to wrist to the nock of the arrow. This will necessarily mean that the draw hand moves away from your head and then back in as you come to your reference point.

The other muscles in your forearm which you will want to use—flexor digitorum—are those which close the fingers and thus hold the bowstring. These only stay tense until the moment of release. At that point (see the chapter on technique) you just relax those muscles—you don't open your fingers, you merely stop forcing them tight and let the bow do the rest of the work.

At this point I should say as strongly as I can that, in the event of any archery-related injury, seek help from a qualified first-aider. Should you experience any unexplained pain in either bones or muscles, get advice from a suitable sports physiotherapist or doctor. I would also advise you, should you suffer any injury outside archery, to consult a physiotherapist or doctor before continuing archery since such an asymmetric sport can exacerbate injuries.

More muscles you won't want to use if you can possibly avoid doing so are the facial muscles. Changing the shape of your face through pouting at the string, pulling other faces, or closing one eye if you don't have to will all affect the position of your anchor reference point and thus the result of the shot. Consistency is the key and thus total relaxation of muscles that aren't needed to be tensed is key. Also, don't chew gum while shooting. Your jaw moves!

DEVELOPMENT

As a child enters puberty and adolescence, there are several changes which occur of which archery coaches and parents or guardians should be aware.

The skeleton develops throughout a child's growth, ending only some years after they stop growing. Bones develop from the ends rather than the middle, just where most stress is placed on them by archery. Too much stress before the bone has stopped growing and has hardened will damage it permanently. Children's bones are particularly vulnerable during growth spurts such as in puberty. Furthermore, while the adolescent growth spurt precedes muscle (and therefore strength) development, development of the skeleton continues after muscle development stops (not reaching full bone hardening until about age 21 in boys, 18 in girls), so merely being able to pull a given draw weight is no guarantee at all that they should be pulling that weight. By the end of a beginner's course, I would not let a child younger than 13-14 years old use a bow more than 16 lbs draw weight, and a grown man of only average build and fitness should not pull more than 22 lbs.

Girls develop ahead of boys, and are generally fully grown by about 15-17 years old. For boys, full growth is normally only reached at about 18-19 years old. Once they are past that, and provided they have reasonably good fitness and archery form, increases in bow draw weight can be introduced gradually. A jump of more than about 4 lbs will probably in most cases prove too much.

Let me make this crystal clear: Overbowing a junior archer is a surefire way to cause them injury and possibly permanent damage.

EYE AND BRAIN

The human brain is a funny thing. As I explain in the chapter on technique (see the section on aiming), when aiming, the preference is to keep both eyes open. If this can't be done, then covering the inoperative eye is the next best option.

Why the brain should react one way when one eye is covered and another when it is closed, I can't fathom, but I have it on good authority that this is how it behaves.

Similarly, string picture can move around depending on lighting. Once again, refer to the chapter on technique. You will need to be conscious of this if you start shooting in the morning with the sun on one side and, after a nice lunch of sandwiches and fruit juice, continue with the sun on the other side of the field and find that your arrows are now consistently going off to one side. Field and 3D archers, who may shoot in different directions on different targets within one event need to be particularly aware of this phenomenon.

DISABILITY

Archery is an excellent sport for disabled people to enjoy as a look at footage from past Paralympics will show. Allowances and arrangements can be made for all sorts of disabilities, for wheelchair users, those lacking one or both arms, deaf archers, and even blind archers. The British Wheelchair Archery Association helps promote para-archery and assists with all aspects of the sport from grassroots. See their website and those of other organisations dedicated to helping disabled archers in the list of links at the end of the book.

CHAPTER 6

TECHNIQUE

BOW ASSEMBLY

This is an area where some people for some reason have difficulty. Whether provided with a table for assembly, or doing it at the back of your car or on the floor of an indoor range, this section should help you.

Start with assembling your bow stand and use it throughout. I've seen archers get into so many problems juggling string, riser, limbs, and sight through not taking the simple step of leaving the riser on the stand.

1. Put the riser on the bow stand, belly downwards, orientated the same way each time. (I'm right-handed and put the top of the riser to the right every time. This enables freeing the right hand to manoeuvre the top loop of the string.)
2. If you use the type of bow sling which attaches to the riser, put it on now.
3. Identify the top limb and attach it to the riser. Limbs should either be labelled for easy differentiation or, alternatively, often the top limb will have no labels or logos on the side facing the archer.
4. Attach the bottom limb.
5. Put the top loop of the string on the top limb and slide it down the limb past the nocks. For easy identification, the top loop should be larger than the bottom, and the nocking point should be closer to the top of the centre serving than the bottom. Ensure that you don't put extra twists into the string or let twists unwind. You should be using a clip to keep the ends together or putting

one end twice through the other when the string comes off and goes into your bag. Then put the bottom loop of the string on the bottom limb.

6. Put the stringer on the bow, the pocket of the stringer on the bottom limb tip, the loop of the stringer over the top limb tip and down past the loop of the string.

7. Take the riser off the stand and place one foot (or both if necessary) on the slack part of the stringer, ensuring you don't also snag the string itself.

8. With the hand closest to the bottom limb, grasp the riser at the grip and place your other hand on the top stringer loop. Pull the riser upwards, and as you do you will be able to transfer your hand from the stringer to the top loop of the string, until you can slide the top loop into the nock on both sides of the limb.

9. Release upwards pressure on the riser slowly and gently, ensuring as you do so that the string is in the grooves at the end of both limbs.

10. Take your brace height gauge and clip it to the string adjacent to the nocking point on the centre serving and check your brace height from string to either the throat of the grip or to the centre of the button plunger. If the brace height has changed from last time you shot, you will need to unstring the bow (I would suggest only at the top) and either add twists (to increase the brace height) or take twists out (to decrease brace height), then restring and recheck brace height.

11. Having achieved the correct brace height, put the bow back on the stand and attach any sight, stabilisers, button, dampers etc. that are removed for storage.

DISASSEMBLY

Disassembly is simply the reverse of assembly. Once again, use the stand—it helps!

1. Put the bow in the stand and remove stabilisers, dampers, sight, and button. As you do so, put each item in your bag. It frees up hands and stops small items rolling on the floor to be lost, claimed by other archers, or coated with mud.

2. Put the stringer on the bow, loop at the top, pocket at the bottom.

3. With a foot or feet on the stringer and hand closest to the top limb holding the stringer loop in place, pull up with the other hand.

4. Slip the top loop of the string out of the nocks and slide it down the limb towards the riser.

5. With your spare hand on the loop of the stringer to stop it suddenly slipping down the limb, gently relax the upward pressure with the other hand.

6. Bow goes back in the stand.

7. Take the stringer off the bow and put it away.
8. Take the string off, secure the ends so that you preserve the number of twists, and put it away
9. Remove limbs one at a time and put them away.
10. Put riser and stand away.

And before you pick the bag up and sling it over your shoulder, ensure you have fastened it or zipped it up! (Learn from other people's experiences!)

WARM-UP

Even if you shoot every day, even if you lead a very active life, I strongly recommend you warm up every time and follow a routine similar to the following each time you shoot. Start from the ground up, paying particular attention to the upper body—shoulders, neck, and arms.

If for any reason of disability or infirmity any of these exercises are difficult, find a suitable way of modifying them, or leave them out. The intention is to prevent injury, not promote it!

Feet and Ankles

Standing on one leg, rotate the other foot around a vertical circle five times in each direction. Repeat for the other foot.

Hips

With hands on your hips, swing your waist around in a circle as if using a hula hoop. Do this five times in each direction.

Arms and Shoulders

With elbows at your side and hands at your shoulders, swing your arms downwards and backwards, then back up as if using ski poles. Repeat ten times.

Begin with arms straight out to either side and palms of your hands facing down. Rotate your hands backwards so that your hands are palms up. Rotate forwards again to the starting position, then repeat ten times.

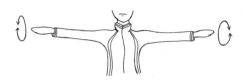

With arms straight out to either side, make circles with your hands in each direction. Repeat ten times.

With arms out horizontally to the sides, raise both forearms so your arms make the shape of an L, hands up and facing front. Lower one hand by rotating your forearm downwards as far as it will comfortably go, then back up. Repeat with the other hand. Do this five times with each arm.

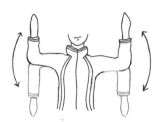

With arms out horizontally to the sides, bring your right arm round in a semicircle to the left hand and then draw it back to its original position, keeping the right hand in contact with your arm and chest. Repeat with the left hand, and repeat these movements five times.

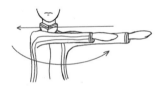

T-DRAW

T-Draw is the name given to the stance and style of shooting for target archery, either with an Olympic recurve bow or barebow. It is also applicable to compound archery but less so to field archery, due mainly to possible differences in terrain. The name comes from the shape the body makes seen from a three o'clock position, with one arm (the bow arm) pointing towards the target and the other (the draw arm) pointing away, with the legs and trunk of the body upright.

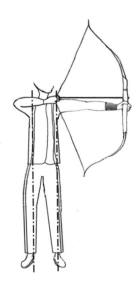

Have a look at the colour photographs of good and bad posture and refer to them throughout this section.

All elements of the shooting sequence outlined next are separate, discrete movements. Don't let one merge into the next, and don't rush any of it.

STANCE

With your bow in the correct hand, place one foot behind, one in front of the shooting line, approximately a shoulder width apart, initially with your toes on an imaginary line going straight from them to the centre of the target. With experimentation, the placing of your feet could change from this neutral stance to one more open (i.e., with your body rotated slightly towards the target). I will cover this experimentation later in the book. Your weight should be distributed approximately 60% on the balls of the feet, 40% on the heels. I also suggest that, until you are completely comfortable with your foot placement, you put a target pin (or tape, if shooting indoors) at the toe of each shoe so you can come back to the same placement at the start of every end. Furthermore, you should keep your feet stationary between arrows, so if using a ground quiver, ensure it is within easy reach before you start.

Your knees should be straight but not locked, so not forced backwards. The intention throughout the shot is to use as few muscles as possible since muscle use can translate into movement—of your body, your string hand, and the bow. In other words, there are two ways of keeping a limb still—one is to have counteracting muscles tight, the other is to have no force acting on the limb at all, or minimal force. This second option is the best method for an archer.

Keep your trunk upright, not leaning towards or away from the target, and not forwards or backwards (along the shooting line), and keep your shoulders down. Your spine needs to be straight. This is an awkward position to get initially, and the movement required to straighten the spine is a sort of slump as if about to sit down, rotating the pelvis (but not pushing it) forward. The net result should be the curve in the small of your back straightening.

This is an ideal element to practise at home in a long mirror. It might help to put lines of masking tape on the mirror. Having achieved this stance, the idea is now to keep your entire body stock still with the exception of shoulders, arms, and head.

STRING HAND

Nock an arrow. You should not handle an arrow by either the nock itself or on the fletches, but only by the shaft. The way I generally recommend is to pick an arrow out of the quiver backhanded (i.e., thumb downwards), bring it over the bow and straight onto the nocking point of the string and then place the shaft onto the arrow rest. As the arrow goes onto the string you should hear an audible click, and the arrow should then stay quite happily on the string unless one of the limbs is given a sharp tap, when the arrow should detach. If none of these happens, find out why, and don't use that arrow until the reason is found and corrected—an arrow that comes off the string prematurely could be extremely dangerous.

One very bad (but quite common) habit is placing a finger of the bow hand on top of the arrow to try to keep it on the arrow rest. Why is this a bad habit? Two reasons. First, because most arrow rests are fragile and quite easily damaged by mishandling by downward pressure this practice provides, and secondly because if the arrow tends to come off the rest easily, the temptation will be to keep the finger there as you draw, and then as you release. Having an arrow through your finger will not encourage use of clean language.

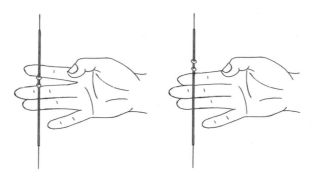

Set your string hand. For freestyle, your index finger is on the string above the arrow, middle and ring fingers below the arrow (see illustration above, left—note that, for clarity, the finger tab is not shown). Ensure that you don't pinch the arrow with your fingers. Ensure also that, if you can't keep both index and middle fingers away from the arrow, it is your index finger rather than middle finger that is in contact with the arrow. This will ensure that you are not lifting the arrow off the rest. For barebow, three fingers below the arrow as per the illustration, and little finger out of the way (see illustration above, right).

Seen from above your string hand, the picture should be as shown in the illustration (shown once again without the finger tab for clarity's sake).

BOW HAND

Setting the bow hand correctly is one of the items that new archers have most difficulty with, and is rarely taught correctly on beginner's courses. It is also the one item that most often causes injury, by the string catching the inside of the forearm of the bow arm.

To get your hand in the correct position, follow these steps:

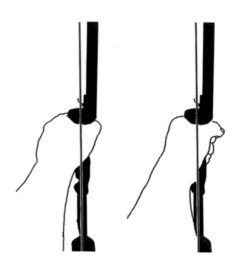

1. Extend your arm horizontally with the hand straight up as if you were stopping traffic.
2. Gradually close your fingers until you can see the outline of the knuckles.
3. Rotate your hand until the line of the knuckles is at 45 degrees to the horizon.
4. The hand should now be in about the same position as that of Adam's, reaching out to God in the painting on the ceiling of the Sistine Chapel.
5. That's the perfect hand position.

The bow should now fit into the U-shape of your thumb and forefinger and rest on that U-shape. That should be the extent of your hold on the bow. So to start with, apply a little tension to the bow with your string hand—not much more than a few centimetres pull. Fit your bow hand to the grip of the riser in the position you found with steps 1–5 above.

The centreline of the grip should now run down the fleshy part of the palm adjacent to the thumb, not down the lifeline. The bone at the base of the thumb (shown shaded in the illustration above) should be on the centreline of the grip. You can now use either just thumb and forefinger to hold the bow, or curl the tip of the forefinger around the back of the grip. You should not be using the rest of your bow hand's fingers to hold the bow as if it were a hammer—you should be able to maintain the 45-degree angle of your knuckles to the horizon. If your hand position is good and the draw weight of the bow anything above about 20 lbs, when you release the bow could well leap forwards out of your hand. This is a good sign, and an indication that you need to use a sling of some variety (see the chapter on equipment). The fingers of your bow hand should not be holding the grip of the riser, nor should they be outstretched, just as relaxed as possible.

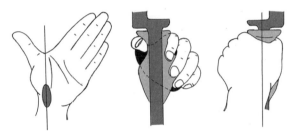

The illustration of the bow hand, which you will have seen in chapter 5 on anatomy, on the left shows a good bow hand, with the line of the knuckles at 45 degrees to the horizon and, on the right, a death grip, with the consequent impingement of the bow string on the archer's arm.

SET POSITION

At the set position (see illustration) you should be facing straight down the line, head upright, with the bow pointing down at about 45 degrees, towards the target, and your draw arm, hand, and the arrow forming a straight line throughout. In this position, to which you should return if your shot sequence is disturbed or you find yourself holding at full draw for too long, you can clear your mind, adjust your breathing, and prepare yourself mentally for the shot.

TURN

Turn your head to the target. Turn just your head, not your upper body or trunk. You should turn your head just enough that you can see the target just over the bridge of your nose, or in cases like mine, just through the upper corner of your glasses.

Don't turn further than that—you should be able to, but if you do, as you draw, your head will move and the main concern here is that, once you have turned your head to face the target, it should not move at all thereafter around any axis.

RAISE

There are several ways to raise and draw the bow, and while I would never suggest that my method is the only correct one, there is one element that is a complete no-no, which is to draw while pointing the bow anywhere near skywards or, indeed, even above horizontal. The only exception here is for field archery where a target may be above the archer. I suggest that readers of this book should follow the instructions below faithfully before experimenting with variations.

Keep both string hand and bow hand at the same height above ground as you raise. While it is acceptable to have your string hand higher than bow hand, for safety reasons the converse is not, and will have others on the shooting line (particularly in competition) protesting at you. Keep arrow and draw forearm in a straight line, thus necessitating lifting your elbow, until your forearm is horizontal, level with your eyes, and your bow hand at the same level pointing in the general direction of the target (once again, refer to the colour illustrations).

An acceptable alternative raise is to bring both hands up higher, so that both are at about the level of your forehead and lower both together as you draw.

Whichever raise you end up practising, breath control is important at this stage. I recommend that people take a full breath in either immediately before the raise or as they raise, and then let half out and hold the rest so they complete the shot sequence on half-full lungs. If there is a danger of you becoming breathless, you are probably taking too long over your shot and should come down and start again.

From the point of view of correct muscle usage, it is important that your draw elbow comes up at the same time as the rest of your arm. If not, there is a danger that you will use the wrong muscles to draw and tire yourself early with consequent degradation in performance early on.

DRAW

Keep the raise and the draw as separate, discrete movements. Drawing as you raise is a bad habit, which will come back to bite if you have any equipment failure or your draw hand slips partway through. So you should never draw at any time that the arrow is not pointing at the target. You would also be using the wrong muscles to draw, resulting in poor technique and tiring early.

The mechanics of the draw are simple—it's not your hand that is drawing the string back, it all comes from your elbow and shoulder, so there should be a straight line from elbow to wrist, down the back of your hand and down the arrow. If you cock your wrist when drawing, you are using muscles in your forearm which will tire, and aren't necessary at all. The intention is to use the larger muscles lower down in the back than at the neck to rotate the entire shoulder rearwards. Once you've come to full draw 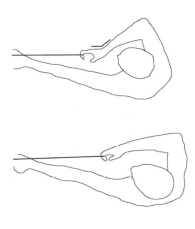 using the wrong muscles with the elbow, wrist, and hand in the wrong positions, it is physically impossible to transfer the load to the correct muscles.

The speed of the draw is important. Snatching at the draw will destabilise your stance and the rest of your bodily position, and drawing too slowly will tire you quickly. You will probably have it about right if you come to anchor within around 1–2 seconds.

ANCHOR

It is important to have a consistent, stable, repeatable reference point at which to anchor your draw hand. If it's not actually in contact with your face, your muscle memory isn't good enough to remember exactly where it is. Your draw hand should come to your anchor point without your head moving at all. I've seen many, many archers place their chin on top of their hand or rotate their head, thus disturbing their early aim. For freestyle recurve archers, the only anchor point should be with your forefinger tucked under the front of your chin, with the string touching chin, lips, and nose. Anchor point will vary for barebow archers depending on distance to the target, but a good starting point is to place the tip of the index finger at the corner of the mouth. Avoid pouting at the string, and keep all facial muscles relaxed.

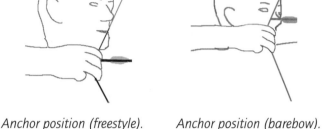

Anchor position (freestyle). *Anchor position (barebow).*

AIM

Aiming is not simply a matter of placing the sight on the gold (or arrow point where it should be in the case of barebow archers). Unlike a pistol or rifle, you don't have a foresight and a backsight. But you do have several different references to use.

Your sighting eye (right if shooting right-handed) should focus on the target. Don't focus on the bow's sight or arrow point. The target should appear sharply in focus to you, and the sight or arrow point slightly fuzzy. Don't try to force the centre of the sight onto the middle of the gold. It might sound counterintuitive, but just allow the sight to float on the gold. Too much stress on centring the sight will bring into play muscles which should be staying relaxed.

To aim, the preference is to keep both eyes open. Some will find this difficult—if their eye dominance is not strong, they might find the wrong eye taking over. In such cases, I don't recommend closing the inoperative eye, but covering it, either with an eye patch, or with a card attached to cap peak or glasses frame. Some people can't get on with this either, and then, and only then, would I say to close the inoperative eye. There are two reasons for this, the first being that if you close one eye, the brain senses 50% of the light getting in, and will dilate the pupil of the open eye to compromise. This reduces your depth of field, which will make the bow sight (or arrow point) appear more blurry and less distinct than before. Oddly enough, if you keep both eyes open but cover one, the brain doesn't react as before, so your depth of field remains as it was. The second reason is that in closing one eye, keeping the other open, you have significant muscle use in your face and, as I have stressed several times, archery is a sport in which we need to use as few muscles as possible.

STRING PICTURE

At this point you also need to check your string picture. This is the blur of the string against either the riser or the upper limb of your bow. It doesn't matter where this is—left of the limb, centre, right—so long as it is consistent. I usually advise archers to use the centre of the limb or riser as most bows have bolts in the top of the riser which can easily be seen and used as references, using the string to bisect the bolt holes.

Changes in lighting can change your string picture, and you'll need to be aware of where the light is coming from. On cloudy days, or indoors with omnidirectional lighting, this won't matter nearly as much. But bear in mind that if the sun is to your right, the left of your string will be in its own shadow and thus will appear darker, therefore the string will appear to have moved left. There will be a tendency therefore to rotate the bow horizontally slightly and for your arrows to land to the left of the aiming point. So you need to be aware of the whole of the string width rather than just the apparent string. A multicoloured string with twists can assist with eliminating this error. It is sensible when making or buying a new string to ensure that the string colour contrasts with the colour of your riser and limbs—a black string is hard to see against a black riser and limbs!

EXPANSION

Expansion is, in effect, a continuation of your draw and becomes more important when you come to use a clicker (also called a draw length indicator; see the chapter on equipment for more information). It consists in a combination of a slight push with your bow arm and shoulder and a slight pull with your draw arm. If you imagine someone's finger between your shoulder blades, then trying to pinch it with your shoulder blades (as your shoulder rotates rearwards with back muscle tension) will provide all the expansion you need. And while, as I say, it is more important when using a clicker, it is sensible to start learning the movement early.

A (repeated) word here about anatomy. The only solid connection of your shoulder and arm to the rest of your skeleton is your collar bone or clavicle. Your arm can, of course, rotate around in a slightly shallow socket at your shoulder or the whole of your arm and shoulder can rotate rearwards from the connection of the clavicle to your breastbone or sternum, and it is this type of rotation that you need to achieve in expansion. It is similar to the sort of rotation of the shoulder you would achieve if you raise your forearm horizontally in front of your face then, without changing the angle of your elbow, pull your forearm inwards towards you.

If you are using a clicker, it should be adjusted so that it clicks about halfway through the extent of expansion of which you are capable. As soon as it clicks, you release.

RELEASE

Don't let go of the string!

The idea is to stop holding it. Yes, I know this sounds odd. But if you just allow the muscles in your forearm to relax from keeping your fingers tense and do nothing else, the bow, the string and the limbs will do all the work for you. Your tab will protect your fingers from string burn, so there's no need to worry about having to get them out of the way. If you actively open your fingers, you will find your forearm rotating outwards, the result being that you pluck at the string, and the arrows go left if shooting right-handed.

You should be continuing the expansion as you release. This will ensure that the tension in your back muscles doesn't relax. As you relax finger tension, you will find the natural tension of your back muscles pull your hand backwards, in a straight line extended from the shaft of the arrow. If it's not straight, the flight of the arrow will be affected. If you pluck at the string in an attempt to get your hand out of the way of the string, the flight of the arrow will be affected, as it will if you do anything other than relax your fingers and pull your hand back. When people have a problem with this, I generally tell them to try to keep their hand in contact with the lower edge of their jaw line, from anchor point below their chin, back along their jaw, keeping in contact, until their thumb ends up somewhere just behind their ear. At the same time, the elbow of the draw arm will probably rotate downwards slightly. This is simply a result of part of the geometry of the skeleton.

FOLLOW THROUGH

The shot doesn't end when you release the string, nor when the nock comes off the string, nor when the back of the arrow clears the riser. The shot doesn't end until the arrow hammers with a satisfying clunk into the gold of the target—or not, perhaps some other part of the target, or misses entirely. So keep still until the shot is over.

Keep still. That's it!

If you have stabilising weights on your bow and a suitable sling, the bow should simply rotate forward until it's pointing at the ground just in front of you. Allow it to do so, using only as much muscle power as is necessary to control the bow's descent. For the rest, you should maintain your posture until the arrow has hit the target. If your hand and shoulder continue to rotate rearwards, then fine—it shows you still have some expansion left after the clicker goes.

But don't overdo either the rearwards motion, or the drop of the bow as I've seen in some archers—you're not in a Hollywood movie so you don't need to overact!

DRAWING ARROWS

Having emptied your quiver, you'll want to go and get them. This is one area which really should have been covered on your beginner's course, but will also bear some repetition and emphasis here to avoid damage to your arrows and those of others and damage to your reputation on the range!

When walking to the target, walk to one side or the other, not straight down the centreline at the boss. There may be arrows on or in the ground, and treading on them will damage them. The nock end of an arrow can hurt just as much as the point if your shin impacts an arrow stuck in the ground. This is, of course, easy to avoid on an indoor range, and there may be limited space between targets. So take care in both directions.

Approaching the target, by all means pick up arrows which have fallen significantly short of the target, by which I mean those more than six feet (2 metres) away from it. Don't pick up arrows closer than that—in doing so you may disturb or damage arrows in the boss.

At the target, in either formal or informal competition, don't touch any of the arrows until all of them have been scored and the scores agreed. Call scores in threes, with a pause between, from the highest score to the lowest, indicating (but NOT touching) each relevant arrow as you do so, for example "9, 9, 7 [pause] 7, 7, 5." If there is a disagreement about an arrow's score, for example whether it has cut the line, ask for a judge (in formal competition) or the opinion of an independent third party. If you are going to compete in more formal competitions, you should really download and read the rules of shooting. You don't need to be able to remember them all, but you will need an idea of what's in there.

Having scored all the arrows, you can then proceed to pulling them. Check with other archers if they are happy for you to pull their arrows as well as your own. Assuming they are, work from the outside edge of the boss inwards.

The technique is to place the flat of the back of your hand which is closest to the boss against the target face with index and middle fingers either side of the arrow shaft. With your other hand, grip the arrow close to your target hand, with your forearm along the arrow (see illustration). Look behind you to ensure nobody is close to the arrow and thus won't get hurt by it, and pull straight backwards. Don't wiggle it loose if it won't come initially, don't push or pull laterally in any direction. If your hand slips and the arrow won't move, you'll need to use your arrow puller on the shaft. If it then still won't move, ask someone else to try, or use an arrow jack. Place the arrow in the hand closest to the target (once again, see illustration) to pull the next.

Once the boss is clear of arrows and you have picked up arrows on the ground close to the boss, distribute all arrows among their rightful owners. You can then go beyond the target to look for any that flew long. Arrows in the ground beyond the target may well have gone in almost horizontally. If you see them, don't just pick them up. Some vegetation, clover particularly, has very strong surface roots and you can easily bend the arrow that way. Pull the arrow out the way it went in. If it's not yours, put it back in the ground, point downwards, standing upright so it's easily visible. If anyone is still missing an arrow, it's considered good manners to help them look for it. If after a reasonable search you are still missing an arrow, don't insist on getting out a metal detector and delaying all shooting until it has been found. That can wait until after shooting has finished for the day.

If you don't return your arrows immediately to the quiver—you may be using a ground quiver—carry them point downwards, with about a thumb's length showing between your fist and the arrow points, with the shafts tucked under your arm. That way you won't injure yourself with either end of the arrow if you should trip and fall. I should, perhaps, at this point emphasise that you should never run on an archery range.

COMMON PROBLEMS

No matter what you do, or how you adjust your sight, the arrow always goes off to the left if you're a right-handed archer.

This is possibly a result of your left eye taking over when aiming. Alternatively (or in addition!) it may be the result of plucking at the string as you release.

The string keeps catching you on the forearm of your bow arm.

Two possible reasons for this are either your bow hand position is wrong and you're gripping the bow, or sometimes in people whose joints overextend, the elbow is bending the "wrong" way. Adjust your bow hand position, ensuring that the line of your knuckles is at 45 degrees to the horizon, or find a way to keep your arm straight.

No matter what you do, even with the sight centred on the gold, your arrows go all over the place.

One significant possibility is not maintaining good positioning during release and follow-through. I've seen bow hands dropping immediately on release, plucking the string to the extent that the draw hand ends up a foot or more out from the archer's face, canting the bow away from the target. One temptation to avoid as much as possible is the desire to see where the arrow has gone. This is the most common reason for people dropping their bow hand or canting it away from the target.

The arrow frequently goes low or falls short.

This is often a result of the draw hand moving forwards just before release, and is sometimes out of fear of the string injuring the fingers of the draw hand. Don't worry about it! You're wearing a tab (or should be) that will protect your fingers. All you need to do is stop holding the string and relax those fingers whilst sliding the hand back along your jaw.

You can't avoid releasing as soon as you come to full draw (i.e., target panic).

Target panic has three main effects. One is that the bow seems to become extremely heavy and makes it impossible for the archer to come to a full anchor position. The second is when an archer finds it impossible to get past a particular point in the shot sequence. The third is as per the heading of this paragraph, and appears to be the most common manifestation of what is called target panic. This is one area that archers of all abilities and experience can find affecting their shooting. The simple answer is that there is rarely a simple answer. My preferred first treatment method as a coach is to work with the archer so that they conduct the shooting of each arrow solely under my instruction, which might be to come to full draw, then wait and come down, or to wait for varying times and release, but not to do any part of the shot without me telling them. This takes the shot sequence out of their subconscious control and returns it to conscious control. But if you find this happening to you, work with your coach.

COOL-DOWN

Using muscles creates waste products in the tissues, predominantly lactic acid. Feeling stiff the morning after unaccustomed exercise is generally a result of not cooling down sufficiently. Cool-down exercises also help develop flexibility and thus avoid injury. These exercises work on shoulder, back, and arm muscles.

Place one hand on the opposite shoulder. With your free hand on the opposite elbow pull upwards just short of the point where it's painful. Hold that position for about twenty seconds. Do the same with the opposite arm, and then repeat each stretch five times.

Place one hand behind your head. With the other hand, pull your elbow backwards, once again stopping short of the painful point! Hold for twenty seconds, repeat with the other arm, and repeat each five times.

Pull your right arm down and across your back, leaning your head towards your left shoulder. Once again, stop just short of the point where it becomes painful! Hold that position for twenty seconds then repeat four times. Switch arms and repeat the exercise for the left arm.

You can modify these exercises as necessary, and different coaches recommend different stretches—all have the effect of helping disperse waste products within the muscle tissues.

ILLUSTRATIONS

Set position.

Turn head.

Raise bow.

Draw.

Anchor: freestyle.

Anchor: barebow.

Release.

Good posture.

Poor posture: leaning back.

Poor posture: leaning forwards.

Poor posture: leaning back.

Poor posture: S-shape back curve.

Arrow retrieval: first arrow.

Arrow retrieval: subsequent arrows.

Seen from above: good alignment.   *Seen from above: draw elbow forward.*

*Seen from above: draw elbow and
shoulder not aligned.*

Stylist riser.

An ILF limb.

Takedown limb.

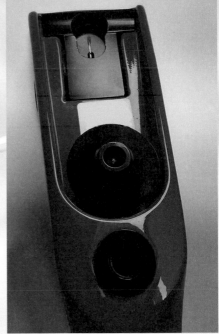

Takedown riser.

An ILF riser.

Stylist limb.

CHAPTER 7

THE MENTAL GAME

It's easy to dismiss the mental aspect of archery. Like many similar precision sports in which one is left alone to carry out what actions are needed in relative peace undisturbed by competitors, such as shooting, snooker, darts, golf, or croquet, the mental element controls the physical and thus it is important to have some familiarity with what it can do.

I'm not going to go into this in any great detail, but just enough (I hope) to help an intermediate archer get that little bit further towards whatever goal they've set themselves.

PREPARE

Yes, I know it sounds obvious. But one of the beauties of archery is being able, hopefully, to put outside worries and concerns behind you at the field. I leave my phone on silent, and in my car when at the range. I don't want hassles from outside. Whether competing, when concentration is important, or simply shooting on my own at the range for my own enjoyment when I want the peace and solitude, having outside concerns doesn't help, nor does being reminded of them. In this respect, therefore, there is a lot of zen attached to the practice of archery.

So put things you don't need to worry about right now out of your mind. The car needs servicing? Offspring not doing well at school? Phone running out of credit? Why worry about these when shooting? If you can't put them out of your mind at all, go away and address them, sort them out, and then come back.

Empty your mind of all except the shoot.

I'm not going to address anyone whom I coach as grasshopper! (If you know, you know!)

ADMIT IT'S YOU

You control the bow. Nobody else. I am frequently asked "Why did it do that?" when an arrow goes astray. It didn't do anything. You made it do that. Accept it. When things go right, acknowledge them, pat yourself on the back (you deserve it!), and try to repeat whatever it was. When things go wrong, tell yourself that something was wrong in what you did, work out what it was, and eliminate it. And subconsciously you may know what it was but your conscious mind doesn't—that is one area in which your coach can help, observe, and analyse. But when you're standing on the line with a bow in your hand, it's just you. So be proud of your good performances, but don't beat yourself up when things don't go right (or rather, you didn't do things right). Analyse what the problem was, and correct it next time. We learn far more from failure than we do from success. I often tell people I'm coaching that there are good results days or good learning days!

Target panic (see chapter 6 on technique) is a form of mental block—it is also ultimately under your control, no matter how it feels at the time. Do something about it. Get some coaching.

DON'T LIKE ARCHERY?

Give it up. Why do it?

There are all sorts of reasons people get satisfaction out of archery—for the satisfaction of winning in competition, for being better today than you were yesterday, for being able to discipline your mind and body, for the peace and solitude of being at the archery field on your own on a nice sunny morning, or for the camaraderie and social life, the "craic" as the Irish say, of socialising with others with a similar hobby on a club evening or weekend shoot.

But if none of these gives you satisfaction, don't do it. And if it once was fun but has stopped, work out what it was that you enjoyed and get it back. Has the membership of the club changed and it's not as sociable as it once was? Change clubs. Is field or 3D archery getting too strenuous as you get older? Can you find the same fun in target archery instead?

If you really, really want to compete and win and see a silver medal as the reward for "first loser," but that's all you've been able to achieve recently, revise the sort of competitions you've been entering—which entails knowing your own form and limitations.

SET GOALS

Ever heard the acronym SMARTER in relation to goal-setting? It's a useful one. It's useful in two ways. First, it gives you something to work towards, something you know you can achieve. And second it stops you overreaching and setting yourself up for disappointment. So what is it?

S—Specific

The goal needs to be clear and specific in order to focus your efforts or to achieve it. When drafting your goal, consider exactly what it is—"improve my scores" doesn't cut it. "Score an average of 280 over 6 ends" is specific.

M—Measurable

"Demonstrate good form on every arrow" is not measurable. A specific (there's that word again) improvement in form (e.g., keeping feet stationary throughout an end) is. Winning a medal in such-and-such a competition is.

A—Achievable

Winning the county championship is probably not achievable in your first year of archery. But what is achievable for you can be the subject of a conversation between you and your coach.

R—Relevant

There is no point to a goal which is not relevant to your ultimate aims in archery unless there is direct relationship. So, "finish my degree thesis by April to concentrate on archery practice" is relevant. This, however, is only an intermediate goal.

T—Time-limited

Every goal needs a target date, so that you have a deadline to focus on and something to work toward. This part of the SMARTER goal criteria helps to prevent everyday tasks from taking priority over your longer-term goals. A time-limited goal will usually answer these questions:

- ≫→ When?
- ≫→ What can I do six months from now?
- ≫→ What can I do six weeks from now?
- ≫→ What can I do today?

E—Exciting

Here's where the inspiration sets in. If you can say "Hey, wow! Getting there would be quite something!" about your goal, it qualifies.

R—Recorded

If it's not recorded, it didn't happen. If you plan to shoot 600 arrows every day for a week as part of your goal, perhaps with a total score in mind at the end, get someone else to witness it. Get the result published in an archery magazine. Post a photo on social media.

There are other acronyms that might help you in your goal-planning. Both relate to your planning for achieving your goal—TEMPO and GROW.

T—Technique

What changes are needed to your technique? How will you sort that out? Who will help?

E—Equipment

Do you have all the equipment you need? Where can you get it? Can you afford it?

M—Mental

Get yourself in the mindset needed. If you keep thinking "I'll never get this done," then you won't. "I need to work out how I'll get this done" is better.

P—Physical

What are the physical requirements? Are you fit enough? Do you need a specific fitness trainer? Go to a gym? Are you medically well enough?

O—Organisational

Discipline yourself to ensure your organisation is good enough. If you're going to a competition, is all your equipment in good condition? Loaded in the car the night before? Hotel booked? Know how you'll get there? Who will feed the cat?

G—Goals

Set intermediate goals for yourself. If you aim to win a particular competition, which other competitions in the meantime will help you gauge progress? If a new set of limbs is needed, by when will you earn the money to pay for them?

R—Reality

Make sure you are critical of yourself and exactly where you are right now. If you haven't achieved a score of 600 on a round, but only 595, 596 and 590, don't tell yourself "Well, I'm as good as there, so I'm there." You're not.

O—Obstacles

Be prepared for them, be prepared to meet them. Winning the Exshire County Championship is a nice target, but there are significant obstacles—such as every other archer with the same intention. So perhaps modify your goal a tad. Your car being on its last legs with no money to replace it yet could be another obstacle. Prepare for it. Meet it, and overcome it. The most common obstacles, of course, are a job, family commitments, money, and time.

W—Way forward

There always is one. Occasionally, the only way forward may be to ditch your goal upon the realisation that you're not going to make it. Use the experience, learn from it—it's all progress. Use it to set a new goal.

None of this is compulsory. You are allowed to enjoy archery without the intention of setting world records! If you want to stretch yourself, if you want to feel inspired, set yourself a goal that will do for you what you want. If it only gets you to say

"Meh—well, that's okay", and that works for you, then fine. If you want to be able to say "Hey, am I proud of myself or WHAT!?", then use a few tools to help you.

VISUALISATION IN PRACTICE

Visualisation is a good form of practice when away from the range. I sometimes get people I'm coaching to do a visualisation exercise and write it all down.

It consists of imagining yourself on the line, with a bow in your hand, and taking yourself all the way through the shot sequence. It comes down to detail—to the smallest extent of detail.

So when you're standing on that imaginary line, what can you see? The grass? The line itself? How does that chalk mark look? Has it faded slightly? What can you hear—other archers? Voices? Birds?

You take an arrow out of the quiver. Can you see the colours of the fletches in your mind's eye? Can you feel the temperature of the shaft in your fingers? Can you hear the slight click as you nock it?

Fast forward (for the sake of space on this page) to being at full draw. What are you going to look at, think about, check, and plan? As I come to full draw, I check I've come to my consistent anchor point, that my finger is firmly against my jaw and that my head hasn't moved as I draw. I plan the release and follow through, the movement of my string hand rearwards but tight in to my head and the fall away of the bow forwards and controlling it with my bow hand, whilst keeping everything else still. I look at my string picture out of the corner of my eye, and correct my hand and arm if necessary. I assess my breath control, whilst carrying out a mental count—if I get to more than a slowish five, I come down and restart. I let the sight float over the gold and holding it there, start my expansion, telling myself as I do that the clicker will tell me when I've reached my release point at my full draw length, and to be ready for it, as I don't want the clicker to fire before that, as I control it, not vice versa. And when it clicks, I release and carry out everything I had planned. And as the bow comes down and I relax; then, and only then, do I look at where the arrow went.

And I can visualise all that and I can even see, in my mind's eye, where the arrow went. Practising this visualisation helps me to run through everything for real when I'm actually shooting for real.

I GOT RHYTHM

Keep it. Get someone to time you as you shoot. Keep the timing of each shot the same. To help you to do this, make each action deliberate and separate from the next (as I stress in the section on technique). Keep it relaxed. You do NOT want to feel you are rushing, particularly at the end of a long, tiring shoot. If you have to come down, don't just go straight back to the raise. Have a brief pause, wiggle your head and shoulders, look at the sky, then get back in the groove, and by this time you should be raising the bow at about the same time as you would had you shot instead of coming down.

I CAN DO IT WITH MY EYES SHUT

Yes, you can. If you find your subconscious taking over, disturbing your shot, killing concentration partway through, spend a practice session up close to the target (about 5 yards), and shoot with your eyes shut. Do everything except actually aiming, and, with your eyes shut, you can concentrate on every aspect of the process.

HOW DID YOU SHOOT?

This relates to admitting it's you. The answer is always "fine" (unless it's "brilliantly!"). If the results on the target were not what you wanted, then tell yourself that you had a good learning experience. It's positive! Don't make excuses. If an aircraft flying low put you off, get back in the groove. It's you in control. Don't surrender control to outside forces, or you'll never win. But if, Zen-like, you shut out everything else and you practiced (or competed) under control all the time, no matter what the result, you did well. You either did exactly what you wanted to achieve (or possibly more), or you learned. Either is fine. Or brilliant.

CHAPTER 8

BEHAVIOUR AT THE RANGE

These rules are not there simply for the sake of it. Misbehaviour may get you thrown out of a competition, or simply make you unpopular at a club. Believe me, if you get well into the sport and are dedicated to improving your performance and scores, you will appreciate others following these guidelines!

SAFETY FIRST

Safety should be your number one concern at all times on the range, not just for your benefit but also for those around you. Don't run anywhere on an archery range. Never use earphones or headphones to listen to music or podcasts, to take phone calls or for anything else—and don't talk on the phone on the shooting line!

Ensure you know and are familiar with all whistle and verbal commands. Some clubs use slightly different protocols. For example, in the case of a shout of "FAST!", while it is accepted that you should remove the arrow from the string and replace it in your quiver, some clubs ask archers to step back from the shooting line to behind the waiting line, making it easier for the Field Captain to see if there is anyone who has not heard. If you see that someone else has not heard the "FAST!", then repeat it to them loudly. Note that a deaf archer should have someone working with them who will throw an object such as a towel in front of the archer as a substitute for the verbal command.

Always point your bow downrange (toward the target) when your bow holds a nocked arrow.

Don't draw a bow, with or without an arrow nocked, except with the bow pointing downrange.

The shooting line is the only place on the range that a bow and arrow should come together. Anywhere else on the range, do NOT nock an arrow. Likewise, never nock an arrow when anyone else is downrange.

Never cross the shooting line for any reason when others are still shooting, and never shoot from behind the shooting line.

Do not drink alcohol anywhere at the range. Similarly, do not use any other drugs or substances, whether legal or not, which alter perception or reduce muscle control.

DRESS

Dress appropriately—not just out of respect for others, but also for safety. Therefore, long hair should always be tied back.

Remove large earrings—anything except studs in the ears should be avoided—as should any facial studs which may contact the string.

Hoodies are popular now and strings around the hood should be tucked well away.

Open-toed shoes are a complete no-no. So do not wear sandals, flip-flops, or any other type of shoe which leaves the toes unprotected. This should also apply to any visitors or friends who come to the range with you.

CONSIDERATION FOR OTHERS

Do not talk loudly while others are shooting or talk to another archer who prefers to be silent.

Do not smoke (or vape) on the shooting line or the waiting line.

Don't offer advice to another archer unless asked.

Stay behind the waiting line when not shooting (unless you're helping an archer with their form).

Don't shoot distances beyond your capability or that of your bow to avoid continually missing and holding up shooting.

Know how many arrows you have shot and how many are in your quiver.

Take into account other archers shooting on the same target when positioning foot markers, and allow sufficient space for them.

Don't disturb people with loud mobile phone ringtones or speaking on the phone on or around the shooting line.

While you may see people wearing t-shirts saying "Aim, shoot, swear, repeat," be aware that exclamations on the line may be a distraction to others. If you swear or exclaim loudly at your performance during a competition, you almost certainly will find people complaining about your behaviour.

Have consideration for other archers, particularly when approaching or leaving the shooting line, as you may distract others. If shooting indoors, be aware of space around you as well, and take care not to bump others or their equipment. Pay attention to how many arrows others shoot. If they often wait for you to shoot your arrows before they can retrieve theirs, you should shoot a bit faster or, if this is not practicable, take fewer shots. You don't have to shoot every arrow in your quiver.

Keep your bow vertical (upright) and in front of you at all times while on the shooting line. Don't rotate it to the horizontal to nock an arrow, or allow the lower end to wave around behind you, as it may well interfere with another archer.

Don't join or leave the shooting line if the archer next to you is at full draw, but stand still until their arrow hits the target. It is also considered good manners not to leave the last archer on the line alone.

Don't leave litter—someone else has to clear it up!

OTHER ARCHERS' EQUIPMENT

Never touch anyone else's equipment without permission. If you break another's arrow through carelessness, offer immediately to pay for it on the spot.

FRIENDS, RELATIVES, AND OTHER ANIMALS

If you take a dog with you to an archery range—and quite a few dog owners do—you will need to be responsible for its behaviour. A well-behaved dog is often very welcome. My own club has a water bowl specifically for visiting dogs. However, one that isn't well-behaved is a distraction to everyone. If they are inclined to wander towards the targets, shooting will have to stop. If tied up and whining or barking, they will distract. If your dog is likely to behave like that, it is kindest to leave it at home.

Friends and relatives also need to understand that it is easy to distract other archers by loud conversation, by making audible comments or asking questions. They also need to be clear that they must not go forward of the spectator line (if there is one) or cross the waiting line at any time. They might, with permission of the field captain, if there is one, go to the target with you when the range is closed for shooting, but ensure they are familiar with how and where to walk, and to beware of arrows that might have fallen short. If they damage anyone else's equipment, you must offer immediately to pay for it. In short, it is probably easier if they sit in a chair and enjoy the sun!

IN COMPETITION

Note the guidance above on dress at the range, and also note the rules for dress in competition, such as a ban on bare midriffs, denim jeans, or camouflage pattern clothing or equipment. Many competitions will enforce the rules strictly, other less formal competitions not so much. Be aware of what will be expected—if in doubt, contact the event organiser beforehand.

Don't touch any arrow until all scores have been recorded and agreed.

Don't touch anyone else's arrows without permission. Ask whether it is okay to draw the arrows once scoring is complete. When drawing other archers' arrows from the target do so with as much care as if they were your own. The exception to this rule is when the arrows are found in the grass. The correct procedure there is to draw the arrow carefully out of the ground and stand it point down in the ground where it was found.

Don't go behind the target to retrieve your arrows before your score has been recorded.

Don't walk up and down the shooting line comparing scores.

When calling scores, do so in groups of three, highest score first (e.g., "7, 7, 5 [pause] 5, 5, 3"), pointing at (but not touching) the nock of the relevant arrow as you do so. Scores must be recorded in this order, so to call your arrows in anything but descending order of score is being inconsiderate of the target captain.

Thank the target captain at the end of each round for their work. And thank the field captain at the end of the day!

CHAPTER 9

COMPETITION

Many archers practise the sport simply to enjoy the open air, to see their personal performance improve, for the social aspect, and for the effect on their physical fitness. However, many also compete, in club competitions, between clubs in the local area, or at county or national levels. Such competitions are often open to all ages and all abilities, with a handicapping system, so no archer should feel they are not experienced enough to compete.

SCORING

There are two methods of scoring in target archery. In general, a competition format in which scoring is according to the imperial method will be shot at a distance measured in yards, while one scored according to the metric system will have distances in metres.

Imperial scoring   System of scoring in which each colour of the target scores only one value: gold = 9, red = 7, blue = 5, black = 3, white = 1

Metric scoring   System of scoring in which each colour is divided into two scoring zones, 1–10

If you take a close look at a standard 122 cm target face, which you will quite possibly have met on your beginner's course, you will see that there is a further ring inside the 10-ring. This extra ring is called the X-ring. Inside that is a small cross (nicknamed the spider) which has no scoring function at all but simply marks the dead centre of the target and should be 130cm above ground level. As stated in the chapter on technique, call scores in threes, with a pause between, from the highest score to the lowest, indicating each relevant arrow as you do so, for example "9, 9, 9 [pause] 7, 7, 5."

Doz							End Total							End Total	Doz Score	Hits	Golds	Run Total
1	9	9	9	7	7	5	46	9	7	7	5	5	5	38	84	12	4	84
2	9	9	7	7	7	5	44	9	7	7	7	7	7	44	88	12	3	172
3	9	9	9	7	5	0	39	9	7	7	5	3	1	32	71	11	4	243
													Totals	243	35	11	243

On the scoresheet for six ends shown here, you can see the score you just called in the first line on the left with the total for that end of 46. The second end is to the right of that with an end total of 38, which gives a total for a dozen arrows of 46 + 38 = 84, with twelve hits on the target, four hits on the gold, and the running total of 84. The second line shows a score of a dozen arrows across two ends of 88 which, added to the previous line's total of 84, gives a running total of 172. In the last two ends on the bottom line, the archer's performance dropped off a little (perhaps through tiredness) and in the fifth end had a complete miss with one arrow, scoring zero, so the number of hits shows only eleven for that dozen.

COMPETITION FORMAT AND ROUNDS

The format for the competition itself is decided by the competition organisers and published well in advance. It is usually according to one of the rounds specified in Archery GB's Rules of Shooting or World Archery's Rules of Shooting, which will state how many arrows are to be shot at which distances.

For example, a Windsor round is three dozen arrows to be shot at each of 60, 50, and 40 yards for a total of 108 arrows, while a Warwick 30 round is two dozen at 30 yards and two dozen at 20 yards. A junior archer can shoot in any category they feel able to handle for their age and above, or younger, but may not win any awards in a lower category.

Keep a record of initial sight markings for different distances with you. Some people keep it on a mobile phone. I prefer to keep a laminated card in the pocket of my quiver with sight settings written in sharpie pen, just in case of technological failure (e.g., flat battery or phone fallen in the bath). Note that these will only ever be initial sight settings—weather on the day, wind, air density, and humidity can all affect how your sights need to be set, but you need to be able to set to the approximate right area quickly as only one end of sighters is permitted in most competitions. If your settings are good, then whatever adjustment you need to make for the first distance will approximate the change needed for subsequent distances.

Talk to other members of your club, particularly the more experienced archers, to find out about competing and specific competitions. You will find them very willing to help and advise.

PRIOR PREPARATION

Sort out your diet well before the event. Eat a diet balanced in carbohydrates, fats, fibre, protein, vitamins, and minerals. The following table shows example figures for women—for men the need will be higher. On the morning of the competition, it is advisable to have a good meal which includes complex carbohydrates such as brown bread for slow energy release. Avoid a large meal during the day. At the end

Nutrient	Function	Sources	Daily requirement
Carbohydrate	Energy	Whole grain cereals, flour, bread, rice, corn, oats, potatoes, vegetables	300g
Fat	Energy and insulation	Vegetable oils, nuts, animal products	65g (20g of saturated)
Protein	Growth and repair	Meat, fish, cheese, pulses, eggs	50g
Fibre	Healthy digestion	Bran (wheat, oat, and rice), wheat germ, cauliflower, green beans, potatoes, celery, etc.	25g
Water	Transportation, hydration	Most food and drink without added sugar, caffeine, etc.	2 litres
Vitamins and minerals	Regulation of the body's metabolic functions	Most from fruit and vegetables, some (e.g., B12) from animal products	Trace amounts

of the day and within two hours of finishing, have another good meal to replenish and refuel.

Ensure all your equipment is available in your bag the night before, as I am sure you will have checked it is all serviceable. Take any spares that might occur to you, and some that might not. I know two archers (at least) who even take items like spare sights to competitions. If the event is far away, you may well have to stay overnight. Book hotel rooms well in advance, as pressure on them will be high from other archers, officials, their friends, and families.

Keep practising in the week before the competition. Practise with two arrows per end more than is required for the event. If your performance in practice dips, don't worry about it. Certainly do NOT make any significant changes to your technique, rhythm, or routine. It takes about 1,000 arrows to drill changes into conscious and subconscious systems, and the week before an event is far too late for that. Just try to analyse calmly what you did wrong and address just that one area.

WHAT TO TAKE AND WEAR

For the competition itself, ensure you plan ahead to arrive at least an hour before the actual start time—you will need to register, orientate yourself, assemble your equipment, and warm up before the assembly. Ensure you take all your equipment including maintenance tools (see the chapter on this) plus spares such as arrow rests, nocks, fletches, piles, etc. Arrows must be labelled with your name or initials, and you should ensure you have enough for the format of the competition plus a couple of spares just in case.

You will see many people with small tents—the pessimists for shelter from rain, the optimists for shade and respite from the heat. If you take one, put it up only where permitted. Camp chairs are a good idea, as being able to sit only on the ground is tiring.

For competitions in the UK, archers must take their Archery GB membership card. There will be other rules elsewhere, so make sure you know them.

While this is a repetition of the guidance in the chapter on behaviour at the range, it bears emphasis—it is a good idea to check all the rules online for the latest specifications on things like clothing so you can ensure that your clothing meets the rules specified (e.g., no jeans, no camouflage pattern clothing, no strapless tops or bare midriffs, no open-toed shoes).

Dress for the weather. If there is any doubt, have waterproofs available. If the ground is at all likely to be damp, you may need wellington boots. Keep sunblock with you in summer, as well as insect repellent. A hat that doesn't interfere with your shooting is likely to be highly desirable in summer and possibly a woolly bobble hat in winter! In winter also take gloves, handwarmers, and several layers of clothes.

EQUIPMENT FAILURE

It happens. Don't panic! If on the line at the time, take two steps back from the shooting line and attract a judge's attention. This is usually done by holding your bow up in the air—not shouting "JUDGE!" as you may distract someone in the act of shooting. Once sorted out, you will be advised how to catch up with the rest of the field.

Top-flight archers will have a spare bow with them. You are unlikely to! Do make sure you have spare arrows with you. In your preparation for the event, consider how you might address any running repairs needed. Pre-empt any obvious failings such as a string whose serving is loosening or is beginning to fray by replacing it well before the competition, and shooting with it enough beforehand. A spare string is a good idea. Most archers will keep at least a small screwdriver and hex (Allen) keys in a pocket of their quiver.

Arrows which either hang down from the pile in the target or which hit and bounce out require you to stop shooting and call for a judge immediately. In the case of bouncers, it may help you to ask other archers on your target if they saw where it hit. If an arrow hits another and achieves a Robin Hood, the second arrow scores the same as the one it hit. But both will need to be replaced! If through carelessness you damage someone else's arrow, offer immediately to pay for it. In the case of purely accidental damage such as your arrow striking someone else's, there is no need to offer to pay.

FOOD AND DRINK

Most competitions will have food available either free with the entrance fee or paid on the day. If you have specific food requirements such as religious limitations, diabetes, allergies, lactose or gluten intolerance, vegetarianism, or veganism, it would also be wise to check on this before the day and, if in any doubt, take your own food with you. Have suitable snacks with you as well to keep blood sugar levels at a desirable level. Anything high in sugar, particularly refined sugar, is inadvisable. Cereal bars and rice cakes can be good, as can nuts. Slow-release sugars such as are found in bananas or dried fruit such as apricots or raisins are excellent for keeping energy levels up, as are carrots. Keep hydrated, avoiding fizzy drinks, anything high in sugar content, and anything high in caffeine such as energy drinks. While it is very rare, hyponatraemia is a possibility in someone who drinks huge quantities of water, so keep hydrated without gulping litres and litres of water. Fruit juice diluted 50:50 with water is likely to be your best drink for keeping going during the day, and keep sipping it. Chocolate and sweets should definitely be avoided, as should alcohol of course.

DRUGS

Early in your career you are very unlikely to encounter a competition at which drug testing is carried out. It is advisable, however, to know the regulations, especially if you are on any prescribed (or over the counter) medication.

With the gradual relaxation in many countries of laws against use of cannabis, people should be very careful of the need to avoid any foods or diet supplements containing CBD or any other cannabinoid.

The Global Drug Reference Online (Global DRO) provides athletes and support personnel with information about the prohibited status of specific medications based on the current World Anti-Doping Agency (WADA) prohibited list. Global DRO does not contain information on, or that applies to, any dietary supplements, so you need to be very careful with these. Visitors can search the Global DRO for specific information on products sold in Australia, Canada, Japan, New Zealand, Switzerland, the United Kingdom, and the United States.

The UK Anti-Doping (UKAD) website is very helpful in explaining what's banned in sport, and includes areas many people will not have considered such as blood transfusions, and separating out WADA's list divided into substances that are prohibited at all times, those prohibited during the in-competition period only, and those prohibited only within particular sports.

Check the Links section of the book for the websites.

DISABILITY

Disabled archers such as wheelchair users will be able to nominate someone to go to the target to score and retrieve arrows for them. This must be agreed upon before the event starts, and it might be a good idea to check this with the competition organisers even before the day itself. Check also all other facilities and access arrangements for disabled archers if you need to, such as toilet facilities.

HANDICAPS

Your club records officer should keep a note of your competition scores or scores from a club target day and will, from those, calculate your handicap rating. This is then applied in later competition in any rounds shown as handicapped in Archery GB's Rules of Shooting. Note that if you don't have a handicap rating, you cannot enter a handicap shoot.

The processes by which handicaps are calculated and applied are part of the black magic understood by few in the world of archery, and are assessed annually. Check the process with your club's records officer.

FINALLY

Archery is a friendly sport. Don't be afraid of other archers in the competition. Those shooting on the same target as you will be very willing to assist and advise if they know you are an inexperienced competitor. However, in the event of any dispute on behaviour, equipment, scoring, or shooting, you are always entitled to call for adjudication from one of the judges. At some point in a competition format shot over several different distances, targets will need to be moved. It will be appreciated if adults (not juniors!) offer to help with this. Ensure your mobile phone is turned off or set to silent. Do make sure you know and follow the advice given in the chapter of this book on behaviour on the range.

CHAPTER 10

BASIC EQUIPMENT MAINTENANCE

SPARES INVENTORY

In chapter 9 on competing, I briefly mentioned spares you will need to accumulate as you go along.

Here is a list of spares I generally keep:

- Piles
- Fletches
- Nocks
- String
- Tab
- Bracer
- Button
- Sight pin
- Adhesive pads for arrow rest
- Various bolts, especially button plunger grub screws
- Target pins

When coaching, I also tend to have quite a lot of other bits and pieces for running maintenance that I wouldn't expect an archer to carry early on in their career in the sport. You will quickly learn what other items you feel comfortable keeping with you.

TOOLS REQUIRED

For running maintenance on your own equipment you will find it useful to build up a small toolkit that goes everywhere with you when shooting. Nothing is more exasperating than to find that your shoot is to be curtailed for lack of an item.

➣ Screwdriver—I keep a small ratchet-type screwdriver with a selection of interchangeable bits.
➣ Hex key sets—Both imperial and metric.
➣ Brace height gauge
➣ Pliers—Plus pliers with the right size of cutout to crimp brass nocks.
➣ Sharp knife—An art or utility knife with snap-off blade sections is always useful.
➣ Fletching jig—If you have learned to fletch, this is indispensable. Until you have learned, many clubs will be able to lend you one.
➣ Fletching glue—Even if you don't own a fletching jig, a friend in the club who has kindly offered to refletch arrows for you would, I am sure, appreciate not having to use their own glue.
➣ Acetone—If you are going to fletch arrows yourself, get a large (1 litre) bottle of pure acetone. This is the main constituent of nail varnish remover. Do NOT use a specific nail varnish remover, which will have all sorts of extra oils and smells added, which defeats the purpose of using acetone, which is a wonderful cleaner and degreaser of arrow shafts, and without which fletches won't stay on long.
➣ Glue—Any hot-melt glue is fine for aluminium arrows. However, for carbon or aluminium/carbon arrows, ensure you use a low temperature hot-melt glue.
➣ Heat source—A chef's blowtorch is a great source of heat for removing and replacing piles and glued nocks.

MAINTENANCE

String Waxing

A bow string needs to be kept waxed to keep it from fraying. There is a lot of friction between the strands, and between the string and everything else such as your bracer or bow stand. If it does become frayed, replace it as soon as possible. If any strands actually break, do not shoot it again—immediately get rid of that string.

For waxing, you will need tension on the string, so it is usually easiest to do this with the bow strung. Run a wax stick up and down the string, avoiding the servings, so you deposit wax all along the exposed areas of the string. Next, with a small pad wrapped around the string—a bit of soft leather is ideal—rub vigorously up and down until you can feel the heat of friction through the leather. Once again, ensure you avoid the servings. Letting the wax heat up will embed it in between the strands of the string. As it cools, you will feel the string become slightly stiff and thus slightly resistant to bending.

Keep the same number of twists in the string each time you string and unstring your bow. String clips are available from suppliers; some people use a clothes peg or paperclip. I insert one end loop of the string though the other, then pass the second loop through the first. Whichever you do, I advise strongly that you then put the string in a suitable bag or plastic storage tube before putting it away in your bag with all the other bits and pieces.

Serving Replacement

Servings come undone. End servings are problematic to replace and might require binning the string and getting a replacement; centre servings are less problematic. If it happens to you, it is best to replace the serving than to try to secure it. This is something which you can learn in time. At the beginning it would be advisable to leave it to an experienced string maker—your club will probably have someone who can do it. Once you have been shown, it is a fairly simple job to accomplish. You will need a reel of the correct type, diameter (and colour!) serving thread, and a serving tool. Inexpensive ones are available, but difficult to maintain steady tension. If you can buy (or borrow) a more expensive version that, instead of sorting thread tension by the medium of a series of three holes in the base, uses a set of three rollers, all the better.

Nock Replacement

There are different types of nock.

Taper-fit nocks have a hollow in the bottom which fits over a cone on the back end of the arrow, and glues in place. These are common on bottom-of-the-market arrows. You will need glue and a heat source (and pliers to save your fingertips!) to remove and replace these. Heat the shaft (keeping heat away from fletches) to remove an old or broken nock. Clean the taper section of the arrow with a sharp knife or a piece of fine sandpaper. To fit a new nock, heat the cone and the glue, having first identified which way the nock needs to be positioned. If you get this wrong, you will find that the glue sets quickly and you then can't correct the problem without sacrificing the nice new nock.

Internal-fit nocks (also sometimes called G-nocks) have a pin which goes into the back of the arrow tube or into a bushing which is in turn glued into the arrow. These tend to be a very tight fit, and it is wise to use a plastic nock tool to handle the nock to avoid breaking it—do NOT be tempted to use a pair of pliers! Otherwise they are quick and easy to replace, and to rotate so the index fletch is correctly orientated (i.e., perpendicular to the nock for a recurve bow).

Pin nocks fit over a pin fitting which is glued into the back of the arrow. Like internal-fit nocks, they are quick and easy to replace. The pin also provides good protection against Robin Hood incidents with one arrow trying to fit inside another at the target. As above, use a plastic nock tool to replace these.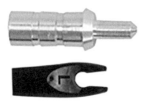

Pile Replacement

This is a job you shouldn't have to do often. It will, however, become necessary occasionally if you make a habit of allowing your arrows to impact the wood of a target stand and burying the point in it. Pull the arrow as normal, and hope the pile stays with the arrow. If not, you will have to dig carefully around in the wood with a stout and sharp knife (I use a Swiss Army knife) to retrieve the pile.

Clean the shaft of the pile as well you can with heat, acetone, and sandpaper. Let it cool—this is important as it will be a tight fit back into the arrow shaft and you don't want heat expansion of the pile. Heat the glue, and spread it around the full circumference of the pile shaft. It's not necessary to use huge amounts of glue, or to apply glue to the full length of the pile shaft. Insert the back end of the pile into the front of the arrow shaft. Then invert the arrow and push it point downwards against a piece of wood or other firm surface so that the pile slides smoothly and quickly into the arrow until only the tip of the pile is clear of the arrow, and all the back end of the pile shaft is inside the arrow. You will probably find a ring of glue around the join of the pile and the arrow. Let the glue cool partly and then you should be able to trim this off easily and cleanly. If it cools completely, it will harden and be difficult to remove at all, and if you don't let the glue cool at all, it will merely smear all over the pile tip and arrow shaft.

Fletching

Fletching is a job which is best learned from watching someone else do it. Ask questions. Learn. There are videos available online which demonstrate fletching, but you can't ask questions, and your jig is probably different.

That said, a few tips which I hope will help:

- I strongly advocate using glue designed specifically for fletching. Some people use ordinary superglue. I find it sets faster than fletching glue, which can be a disadvantage, and the bond doesn't tend to last as long.
- Ensure you have the fletch positioned correctly in the jig's clamp and check the alignment on the shaft before using any glue at all.
- Note that it is very easy to use too much glue and find you have blobs of glue sticking out from under your fletches, or worse, smeared on the shaft, making the arrow unsightly as well as possibly disturbing its flight characteristics. A thin smear on the fletch, such that you can just see light reflected in it, is enough. Some people put little blobs of glue a couple of millimetres apart along the fletch and then even that out with the end of a cocktail stick or toothpick.
- After fletching, allow the glue to harden. An arrow that has just had one (or all) fletches replaced won't have reached the glue's full hardness for 24 hours.
- Don't bother using fletching tape for ordinary vanes. Tape is excellent for spin wings, but tends to come loose from other types of fletch.

BOW TUNING

There are plenty of excellent sources available online for various techniques of bow tuning, for bareshaft tuning, walkback tuning, and paper tuning. I will cover these here for guidance only, since this is something best done under the guidance of an experienced archer or coach. It is helpful that you understand what is going on and why.

I would like to emphasise that the bow, all its attachments, your arrows, and you are all part of a system. Change one element and you will often find yourself having to retune. For example, if you change arrows from one type to another, even with the same fletches, the same nominal spine stiffness and length, you may well find them behaving differently.

Centre-Shot

(Note that the image to the right shows a right-handed bow.)

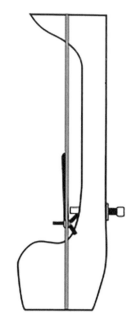

With an arrow on the rest and nocked, look at the string, positioning yourself so that it appears to run down the centre of the riser. The pressure button should line up with the centreline of the arrow, the arrow rest should slope upwards out from the riser, and the tip of the wire rest should only just be visible from above. The arrow should appear to be just to the left of the string as the picture shows, and the tip of the arrow should appear to be tangential to the string.

Adjust as necessary by moving the tip of the pressure button in or out as required. To do this, you will need to loosen two little grub screws on the ring of the button closest to the tip. Don't loosen too much as these screws are hard to find once they fall in the grass!

Put the button back into the riser, and check the arrow position relative to the string again. If it's correct (as shown), remove the button again, and tighten the two grub screws—taking care not to over-tighten—and replace it. Having moved the button plunger, you will probably also need to adjust the arm of the arrow rest.

Set Nocking Point

Use your brace height gauge, clipped to the string, to check where on the centre serving section of the string is the point level with the lowest point of the arrow rest.

If you were to place the bottom nock point so that the top of it were at this point, an arrow would then nock exactly level. However, you will need your initial nocking point to be above that by about 5mm (1/5") so that the arrow is effectively pointing slightly downwards when sitting on the rest.

Put a brass nock on the string at this point, and with nock point pliers tighten to the point where it can still move, but only if persuaded to manually! Your top nock point needs to go slightly more than an arrow's width above that to allow for the closure of the gap when the string is fully drawn. Any less than that and the arrow nock will be pinched. Pinch this brass piece the same as the bottom, and check they haven't moved. Once satisfied that they're both in the right place, you can clamp both as tight as you can get them with your pliers.

I specify using brass nock point indicators at this stage because you may find when you get to finer tuning that you want to move the nocking point in either direction, and I would only recommend tying a thread nock (and gluing it in place!) once you are sure you know where it should be.

Strings

The section below deals with bow tuning, much of which involves fiddling with your string. It is important to maintain the twists in your string once the correct brace height has been found. It is also important, before you make any changes to the string, to note which way any existing twists go! Ignore anyone who tells you "If you're right-handed, you need a right-handed string so the twists go the right way." It's nonsense! To increase the brace height and shorten the string, add twists. To reduce brace height and lengthen the string, remove twists. It's that simple!

Recommended Brace Heights

If you have a manual from the manufacturer of your riser, it should show the recommended brace height range. If not, you can try to find one online, but most risers will be quite happy with a brace height in the ranges shown in the following table.I emphasise that these are ranges. Using the following flowchart, you can find the point where the bow is quietest and thus wasting least energy, and then sort out the right nocking point.

Bow length (inches)	Brace height range (inches)	Midpoint of range
64	7.75-8.75	8.25
66	8-9	8.5
68	8.25-9.25	8.75
70	8.5-9.5	9.0

Using a brace height gauge, you should check the brace height every time you string the bow, having taken care (see chapter 6 on technique) to ensure you don't lose or gain twists in the string each time you string or unstring the bow.

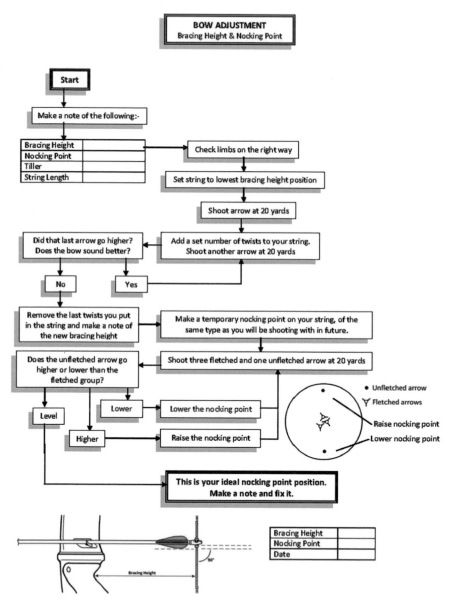

Brace height and nocking point

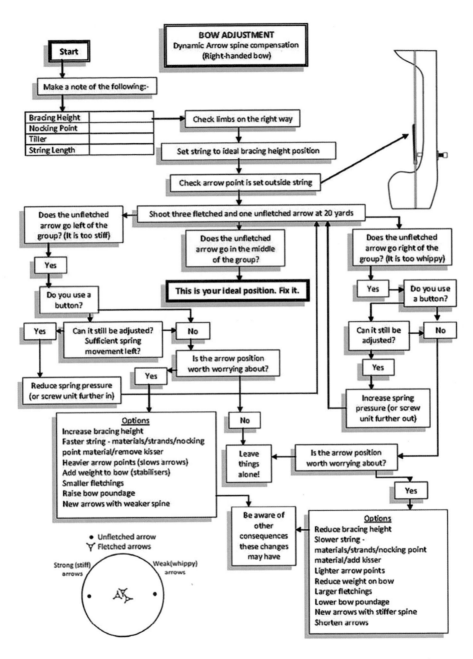

Bareshaft tuning: right-handed bow

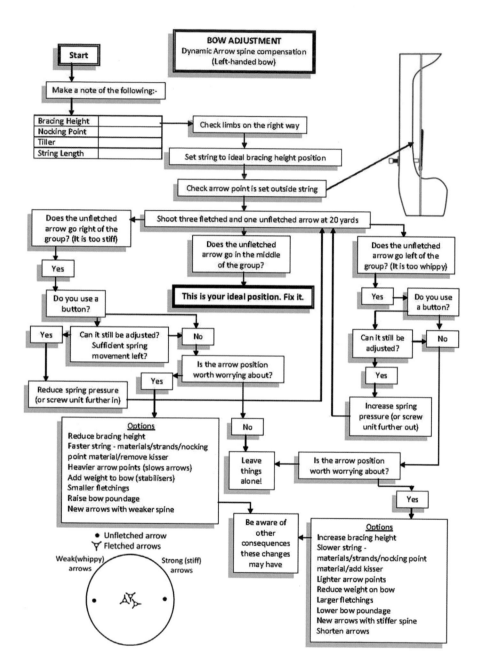

BOW ADJUSTMENT
Dynamic Arrow spine compensation
(Left-handed bow)

Start

Make a note of the following:-

Bracing Height	
Nocking Point	
Tiller	
String Length	

Check limbs on the right way

Set string to ideal bracing height position

Check arrow point is set outside string

Shoot three fletched and one unfletched arrow at 20 yards

Does the unfletched arrow go right of the group? (It is too stiff)

Does the unfletched arrow go in the middle of the group?

Does the unfletched arrow go left of the group? (It is too whippy)

Yes

This is your ideal position. Fix it.

Yes — Do you use a button?

Do you use a button?

Yes — Can it still be adjusted? Sufficient spring movement left? — No

Can it still be adjusted? — No

Is the arrow position worth worrying about?

Yes

Yes

Reduce spring pressure (or screw unit further in)

Increase spring pressure (or screw unit further out)

Options
Reduce bracing height
Faster string - materials/strands/nocking point material/remove kisser
Heavier arrow points (slows arrows)
Add weight to bow (stabilisers)
Smaller fletchings
Raise bow poundage
New arrows with weaker spine

No

Leave things alone!

Is the arrow position worth worrying about?

Yes

Be aware of other consequences these changes may have

Options
Increase bracing height
Slower string - materials/strands/nocking point material/add kisser
Lighter arrow points
Reduce weight on bow
Larger fletchings
Lower bow poundage
New arrows with stiffer spine
Shorten arrows

• Unfletched arrow
Y Fletched arrows

Weak(whippy) arrows — Strong (stiff) arrows

Bareshaft tuning: left-handed bow

Walkback tuning

To start with, prepare a blank target butt. It will help you considerably if there is nobody else trying to shoot when you do this. Use a butt about 40 yards from the shooting line. I recommend setting two targets up, one on the ground resting against the other's stand. Put a target pin in the top target, about 6″ from the top.

With your sight set for 15 yards, walk back five yards from the target and shoot three arrows. Mark the centre of this group with a target pin and remove the arrows. Walk back to ten yards from the target, and repeat. Do the same from 15, 20, 25, 30, 35, and 40 yards.

You should now have a series of target pins in the two targets, making a pattern going down the combined targets in various possible sequences.

If the pattern is a straight line down the target, you have a perfect set-up. Don't mess with it!

The next two possibilities—the pattern of target pins—are a straight line sloping down either to the left or the right. Your centreshot needs adjusting. If the slope is down and to the left, you need to move the button tip right. If the slope is to the right and down, then move the button tip left. Make any adjustments very small—only a couple of millimetres at a time. Note that these directions are the same whether you are right- or left-handed. Note also that moving the button tip may well necessitate moving the arrow rest in or out, but this can wait until you have a straight vertical line.

Two more possibilities—the pattern going down the target curves to one side or the other, the last (bottom) pin more or less vertically below the first. If the curve is to the left, in imitation of the letter C (for a right-handed archer), then the plunger spring tension is too high and needs to be relaxed. If the curve is to the right, button pressure is low and needs to be increased. For a left-handed archer, reverse these instructions. Adjust as necessary and repeat the test.

One last possibility in the pattern of target pins is that you get an S-shape. This indicates that both centreshot and plunger tension are incorrect. Adjust centreshot first before changing button spring tension.

Tiller Adjustment

For efficiency, the limbs have to work in unison. To set the initial tiller adjustment, check the manufacturer's recommendation. If this is not available, for the initial set-up, set the top tiller distance between an eighth and a quarter of an inch (3–5mm) greater than the bottom tiller distance.

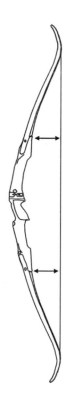

Why this difference? The centre of pressure of the bow is, quite obviously, at the grip of the bow but the arrow rest is above centre, thus the nocking point is also above centre, which has an effect on the power differential of the limbs. To correct this imbalance, a simple explanation is that the lower limb needs to give a little more power than the top limb.

Barebow archers, because of the greater asymmetric effect of string-walking, often use a neutral or negative tiller (when the top tiller distance is less than the bottom tiller distance).

In order to adjust tiller you will probably find that the limb attachment bolts are in two parts and you have to loosen the bolts from the belly of the bow before you can adjust the bolts on the back. If you have the manufacturer's instructions, check those. If not, get someone at your club who knows what they're doing to show you how to adjust limbs. You should end up with limb bolts approximately halfway between free (out) and fully in.

Limb Alignment

String the bow and stand it vertically, positioning yourself so you can see the full length of the string against both limbs and the riser of the bow. Move yourself laterally to where you can see the string lined up with the centre of the top and bottom of the riser. The string should then line up down the centre of both limbs. If not, some lateral limb adjustment will be necessary. Not all risers have this facility where small adjustments can be made to get the limbs in line with the centre of the riser. If yours doesn't, there's not much point in worrying about it!

Limb Twist

To check if limbs are twisted, take a couple of old arrows and slide them between the string and the limb at the end where the two are in contact, just by the groove in the limb, so that the arrow is perpendicular to the string and limb, sticking out on either side. Repeat this for the other limb. The arrows should be parallel to each other. If as you hold the bow, one arrow end is further away from you than the end of the other arrow on the same side, one or other (or both) of your limbs is twisted. An alternative explanation is that the riser is twisted, but this is less likely, and rather more terminal. If your limbs are twisted, once again there's not much you can do about it except replace them.

Finally

Be aware that tuning your set-up correctly is a business that can take weeks of adjustment. The archer, the bow, and the arrows are all part of one whole system, and if you change one thing you will find retuning is necessary to a greater or lesser extent.

Incidentally, some archers advocate paper tuning for recurve bows. I don't. Why? You learn very little if the tuning session is set up correctly, and can learn all sorts of incorrect details which won't help. An arrow shot from a recurve bow will not be flying straight without flexing until it has flown at least nine metres with the largest fletches, further with smaller fletches. Paper tuning is a highly desirable technique for compound bows, but of limited use for recurves.

CHAPTER 11

WHAT NEXT?

Next is to gain a bit of experience, shoot lots, keep in touch with a club coach, get coaching when you can, and learn more about the sport, your equipment, and how to improve.

Thereafter, there are various routes you can take, while still enjoying shooting for your own pleasure. Get involved! Archery in the UK and most of the rest of the world runs on volunteer help. Join your club committee.

YOUR TECHNIQUE

There is a lot you can vary according to taste, result, or through experimentation. I recommend you work with a coach as well as experimenting on your own. For example, you might need to find a better stance for yourself than simply square on to the target. One easy method for this is to stand on the line, close your eyes, and extend your bow arm, adjusting its position laterally until it's comfortable with minimal muscle control and then open your eyes. If your arm doesn't point directly at the target, move your feet until it does. You will now need to place a couple of target pins in front of your toes to mark position for a while until it becomes natural.

There are different raise techniques you will see on the range. Some come straight up to the bow arm horizontal, some raise above that and then lower as they draw. Do NOT, please, follow those few who allow the bow hand to come up above the draw hand so that the bow is pointing upwards. If you do, be prepared to ensure (and point out!) that you are NOT drawing with the bow above horizontal.

If your coach tells you to change any element of your technique, you need to be prepared for an initial degradation in results. It takes time (one estimate is about 1,000 arrows) to ingrain a new item into either muscle memory or the subconscious. Your coach will probably only change one element of your technique at a time and allow you to get used to that before changing anything else. Remember I said that trust is essential between archer and coach? So often people I have been coaching have said "I'm doing what you said, but it's still all over the place on the target," to which my response is "Yes, we changed one thing, but there are another 47 items of your form we still need to work on!" So be patient and continue to work. Be prepared for poorer results at the target initially. I often say "When things are right here" (pointing at the shooting line), "it'll be right there" (pointing at the target). Don't worry about results. They'll come. Work on the form and practise. With any change or adjustment, evaluate the results and discuss with your coach. Read, watch what others do, discuss, and experiment.

COMPETING

One nostrum frequently heard around archery circles is that it is not about being better than the next person, but being better than you were yesterday. However, people are by nature competitive, and competition archery is very popular. By all means compete against others, compete in bigger competitions, and gauge progress that way, if that is what works for you.

COACHING

Coaches and instructors deliver almost all practical, formal training in archery. It can be an excellent way to share your love of the sport, to get more people into the sport generally and your club in particular, and to help the sport continue and flourish. Once qualified at the lowest level as a new coach, there are further training courses that can be undertaken, further and higher qualifications to be gained.

JUDGING

Archery has competitions—competitions need judges to ensure fairness and safety. Just one simple competition on one day can require quite a team of officials, and judging is a good way to participate. Most national organisations specify that judges have to be aged over 18, but can train before that age. You won't be paid, but can generally claim expenses for travel (and hotel if needed), and most event organisers will ensure judges are fed for free!

VOLUNTEERING

Volunteers are always welcome around archery, not just for competitions but also for beginner's courses, corporate events, mundane activities such as field grass cutting, and elsewhere. My own club needs more volunteers than coaches to run each beginner's course. This is a great way to meet new people, to show how friendly the sport is, and to get involved without expense or long-term commitment.

ARMOURER

Most clubs need an armourer, who not only maintains club equipment but can also carry out repairs and maintenance on other members' equipment. The armourer will typically look after the target butts, bows, arrows, and a host of ancillary equipment. They will have a greater degree of knowledge and experience with different types of bow than most archers, and have access to a good set of tools and supplies.

STRING MAKING

Making bowstrings is an art all on its own. A good string jig can be expensive, as can a stock of the materials needed—and in all sorts of colours! Borrowing a jig is therefore probably desirable initially, as well as limiting the colours used. It's another aspect of the sport in which people can help, have fun, and improve their skills—and possibly earn a small amount of money with each string made.

RECORDS

A club records officer has a great deal of responsibility for keeping track of members' performance, scores, classification ratings, and so on. Outdoor handicaps are reviewed annually at the beginning of January and for indoor handicaps at the beginning of July. Archery GB keeps no record of archers' classifications, so a lot falls on the shoulders of the records officer. It is a job which suits someone with good attention to detail, and good record-keeping and organisational discipline.

ARCHER

Yes, you can continue just shooting!

Many clubs operate a badge system such as "252" for different distances for which over 36 arrows in imperial scoring you need to average red (7) or better (gold 9) over the round. Thus scoring a gold means you can afford to drop an arrow into the blue (5). There are other badge schemes around as well by which people can measure progress not just in shooting but also in knowledge of the sport, in technical ability such as how to replace an arrow nock, and more.

You could work towards gaining an archer classification. The specifications for these (for the UK) are in Shooting Administrative Procedures (see Links section) and state what rounds and scores are required for each level of classification. Your club records officer will be able to show you more detail.

You can, of course, shoot just for your own enjoyment if you wish, or compete and aim at improving to the point where you could be selected for club, county, or national teams! Quite a few suppliers and manufacturers also operate their own teams as ambassadors for those organisations, and this is sometimes a great way to get to use the latest equipment for free or at a substantial discount.

SUMMARY

Whichever route you choose, be aware that there are many others to which you could change if you get bored or simply want to try something new within the sport.

I hope you will stay in archery having already taken the first few steps. This book is an attempt to fill a gap, as there are lots of books and other aids out there for the experienced archer fine-tuning their performance and technique, but not much for the early archer who simply wants to know what this, that, or the other looks like. Some new archers feel slightly abandoned once the beginner's course is over. I hope that this book has helped answer many of your questions and provided a bit of guidance.

GLOSSARY

3D—Archery discipline that simulates hunting in scenarios similar to field archery (qv) using packed foam targets of model animals.

aiming point—Spot on the target on which the archer attempts to place the aiming device such as the sight (freestyle archers) or arrow tip (barebow archers).

anchor point (reference point)—The place on your face where your draw hand comes back to consistently each shot.

arrow rest—A device on the side of the riser closest to the archer on which an arrow is placed at the start of the shot cycle.

back (of the bow)—The side of the bow facing the target, opposite to the string.

bale (US)—Target boss.

barebow—Shooting discipline which allows no sights or other visual aiming aid, stabilisation, clicker, or damping on the bow.

belly (of the bow)—The side of the bow adjacent to the string, closest to the archer.

boss—Backing for the target face, to which the paper target face is pinned, often of layered foam or straw, designed to stop arrows.

bow hand—The hand which holds the bow (e.g., for a right-handed archer, this is the left hand).

bow press—Device to take strain from the limbs and cables of a compound bow when replacing parts, adjusting, or restringing.

bow sling—See *sling*.

brace height—Distance from the string to either the throat of the riser grip or the centre of the button.

bracer—Protective shield for the bow arm, usually leather, plastic or similar material, equipped with straps to go around the forearm.

button (plunger)—Device which screws into the riser protruding on the arrow rest side to fine tune both the position of the arrow on the rest and the way in which it leaves the bow when shot.

cable—Part of a compound bow which synchronises top and bottom cams (qv) in reducing draw load as the string is drawn back.

cam—Off-centre wheel on a compound bow which alters the load on the string as it rotates.

clicker (draw check indicator)—Device which attaches to the riser of a bow which makes an audible sound (hence the name) when the archer reaches full draw, thus aiding in keeping a consistent draw length.

cock fletch—See *index fletch*.

come down—Command from a coach or field captain to an archer to relax the draw and lower the bow until the arrow is pointing at the ground in front of the archer.

compound bow—Bow using wheels, cams, and cables to relieve draw force at full draw, providing high power and accuracy.

crawl—Amount down the bowstring that a barebow archer will place their draw hand, varying according to distance to the target.

dominant eye—The eye which the archer (subconsciously) prefers for aiming - not always the same side as the dominant hand

draw—Pull back the string, with arrow attached, to anchor point with the intention of shooting.

draw force line—Imaginary line from bow hand on the riser grip through string hand to elbow of the draw arm.

draw weight—Specified or actual force required to draw the bow a specific distance; limbs are specified with a draw length of 28".

dry fire—To draw fully and release a bowstring without an arrow on the string. Never do this as it damages the bow.

dynamic spine—Extent of the tendency of an arrow to bend in flight varying with draw weight of the bow, weight of arrow pile, shaft length, and a host of other variables.

end—A number of arrows shot at the target before scoring and retrieving them. Normally six for shooting outdoors and three for indoors.

fast—Command to stop shooting immediately. Archers should come down (qv) if drawn, remove arrow from the string, and place it in the quiver. Some clubs insist archers step back behind the waiting line.

Fédération Internationale de Tir à l'Arc (FITA)—Former name of World Archery (WA), the governing body for archery across the world. WA is the IOC's recognised governing body for all archery. Olympic rules derive from the WA rules.

field archery—Archery discipline in which archers walk or run through a course shooting at 2D and 3D targets at unmarked distances, often up- or downhill, often in wooded terrain, and carrying all equipment they might need with them.

field captain—Person designated to control shooting and declare range open or closed. May use verbal or whistle commands.

finger tab (tab)—Protection for the fingers of the draw hand, to provide consistency and smoothness of release. Often made of leather or similar substitute with shaped metal base.

flatbow—Traditional type of one-piece bow with rectangular limb cross-section.

fletch, fletching—Vanes of feather or plastic attached to rear end of an arrow to help stabilise flight and on occasion to provide axial spin.

follow-through—Movement of bow and archer after the arrow has left the bow.

freestyle (Olympic recurve)—Form of shooting complying with WA rules for bows permitting sights, stabilisation, damping, etc. Generally shot with string hand split finger (qv).

Grand National Archery Society (GNAS)—Former name of Archery GB, governing body for target archery in the UK.

grip—The part of the riser which the archer holds when shooting, shaped for comfort and consistency of bow hand position.

International Limb Fitting (ILF)—Specification for attachment of limbs to risers to allow commonality of manufacture

imperial scoring—System of scoring in which each colour of the target scores only one value: gold = 9, red = 7, blue = 5, black = 3, white = 1, with targets usually placed at a specified distance in yards (cf metric scoring).

index fletch (cock fletch)—One fletch of a different colour to help the archer identify which way to nock the arrow on the string.

jig—Device for working with arrows when fletching them (fletching jig), when making bow strings (string jig), or when serving a bow string (serving jig).

limbs—Upper and lower parts of a takedown bow, usually detachable, designed to flex with specified extent and applied force. Marked with draw weight at 28" draw. Also upper and lower parts of a compound bow.

longbow—Traditional type of one-piece bow with D-shaped cross-section.

metric scoring—System of scoring in which each target face colour is divided into two scoring zones, 1–10, usually with targets set at specified metric distances.

nock—Slot in the end of an arrow for fitting to the string. Also double grooves in the outer ends of the limbs to hold the string secure when the bow is strung. Also the act of fitting an arrow to the string.

nocking point—Point on the string where the arrow should be nocked. Often marked by brass rings or thread circles around the centre serving.

Olympic recurve (freestyle)—Form of shooting complying with WA rules for bows permitting sights, stabilisation, damping, etc. Generally shot with string hand split finger (qv).

overbow—For an archer to try to draw and shoot a bow which has too high a draw weight for their size, strength, fitness, etc.

pile (point)—Tip of the arrow, usually removable, either glued directly or screwed into a glued insert.

plunger—See *button*.

power force line—Imaginary line from bow hand on the riser grip along the bow arm through shoulder of the bow arm to the opposite shoulder.

quiver—Container for arrows yet to be shot. This may be attached to the archer by a belt, a ground quiver which stands on the ground in front of the archer, or a clip attached to the bow.

raise—The act of bringing the bow up from pointing at the ground to point downrange at the target.

recurve bow—A bow with limbs curving towards the archer close to the bow hand but in the opposite direction towards the tips.

reference point—See *anchor point*.

riser—The centre part of a takedown bow, including the grip, to which the limbs are attached.

selfbow—Traditional type of one-piece bow (see *longbow*) made from single piece of wood (i.e., not composite construction).

shooting line—Physical line from which archers shoot at the target, with one foot each side of the line. The only place on a range where arrow and bow come together and not to be crossed while shooting is going on.

sling—Device to keep the bow from leaving the hand when the arrow is released, permitting a completely relaxed, open bow hand. May be finger sling, bow sling, or wrist sling.

spectator line—Line at least ten yards behind the shooting line (qv) behind which all non-archers should remain, allowing room for free passage of the archers.

split finger—Shooting with the index finger of the draw hand above the arrow nocking point, middle and ring fingers below.

stacking limbs—Overdrawing a bow, getting the limbs to maximum designed bend or past it and thus risking damage.

static spine—Extent of the tendency of an arrow to bend in testing with a weight hung from the centre.

string—The string stretched between nocks at the outer ends of the limbs, often several strands in a continuous loop with wound servings to protect it at top and bottom and centre where arrow attaches.

stringer—Device to help string a bow, usually with a loop on one end and a pocket or cup on the other.

takedown bow—Traditionally any bow with removable limbs. In modern usage, normally specifying a recurve bow whose limbs bolt on to the riser.

three below—Shooting with first three fingers of the draw hand below the arrow nocking point, generally adopted by barebow archers.

waiting line—Line at least five yards behind the shooting line (qv) behind which all non-shooters should stay.

FURTHER READING

Archery Anatomy, Ray Axford, Souvenir Press, 1995
The Muscle Book, Paul Blakey, Himalayan Institute, 2010
Lifespan Development, Helen Bee & Denise Boyd, Allyn & Bacon, 2014
The Art of Stringwalking, Martin L. Godio, 2019
The Art of Barebow Shooting, Martin L. Godio, 2020
Understanding Winning Archery, Al Henderson, Target Communications Corporation, 1983
Longbow, Robert Hardy, Patrick Stephens Ltd., 1992
Traditional Bowyer's Bible, Steve Allely and others, Lyons Press, 2000
The History of Archery, Theodore R. Whitman, CreateSpace Independent Publishing, 2017
For Maytenance of Archers, E.T. Fox, Lulu.com, 2020
The Archery for Beginners Guidebook, Various, Archery GB, 2013

LINKS

National and Ruling Bodies

All Japan Archery Federation	archery.or.jp
Archery Australia	archery.org.au
Archery Canada	archerycanada.ca
Archery GB	archerygb.org
Archery New Zealand	archerynz.co.nz
British Horseback Archery Association	bhaa.org.uk
British Longbow Society	thebritishlongbowsociety.co.uk
Deutscher Schützenbund	dsb.de
English Field Archery Association	efaafieldarcher.com
Fédération Française de Tir à l'Arc	ffta.fr
Federazione Italiana di Tiro con l'Arco (FITArco)	fitarco-italia.org
International Field Archery Association	ifaa-archery.org
Korea Archery Association	archery.or.kr
Mounted Archery Association of the Americas	mountedarchery.org
UK National Field Archery Society	nfas.net
USA Traditional Archery Society	traditionalarcherysociety.com
USA Archery	usarchery.org
US Field Archery Association	nfaausa.com
World Archery	worldarchery.sport

Archery GB Rules

Rules of Shooting as of 2023	https://archerygb.org/files/rules-of-shooting-240123160956.pdf
Shooting Administrative Procedures	archerygb.org/coaches-judges-volunteers/become-a-judge/documents-guides-forms
Sporting Regulations in the UK	archerygb.org/about-us-structure-safeguard/about-us/governance/policy-and-procedures/sporting-regulation/
Archery GB Coaches' Code of Conduct	archerygb.org/about-us-structure-safeguard/about-us/codes-of-conduct

Second-Hand Suppliers (UK)

Aardvark Archery	aardvarkarchery.co.uk
Clickers Archery	clickersarchery.co.uk
Eagle Archery	eaglearchery.co.uk
Phoenix Archery	phoenix-archery.co.uk
Wales Archery	walesarchery.com

Bow Rentals

Stylist Bows	stylist-bows.com
Urban Archers	urbanarchers.co.uk

Tuning Guides

texasarchery.org/resources/39-tunning

Arrow Manufacturers

Easton Archery   eastonarchery.com

Victory Archery   victoryarchery.com

Disabled Archery

British Wheelchair Archery Association   british-wheelchair-archery.org.uk

Disabled and Wheelchair Archery Clubs for All Disabilities   ableize.com/recreation-sports/archery

Getting into Archery | Disabled People   archerygb.org/clubs-facilities-development/clubs/club-resources/disability-archery

Adolescent Development

Common skeletal injuries in young athletes   pubmed.ncbi.nlm.nih.gov/7747003

Bone Deformation: An Overview   sciencedirect.com/topics/medicine-and-dentistry/bone-deformation

Bone Acquisition in Adolescence   sciencedirect.com/science/article/pii/B9780123705440500318

Anti-Doping

Global Drug Reference Online   globaldro.com

World Anti-Doping Agency   wada-ama.org

UK Anti-Doping: What's banned in sport   ukad.org.uk/athletes/whats-banned-sport-prohibited-list

ABOUT THE AUTHOR

Ben Hastings' interest in archery was piqued at a very young age when allowed to string and unstring (but not shoot!) his elder brother's longbow.

Formerly Ben's target sports were pistol and rifle shooting, but in the aftermath of shootings in Hungerford and Dunblane in the late 20th century, these sports became problematic with increasing regulation and instead his interest in archery was revived with a have-a-go session on holiday one summer. He now regularly shoots freestyle, barebow, longbow and flatbow target archery.

He has been coaching for several years, and is an Archery GB Level 2 licensed coach and Competition Judge. He is a member and senior coach of Farnham Archers, one of the oldest archery clubs in England, having been established in 1870.

Ben coaches archery at a large independent school in Surrey and has also started an after-school archery club at a local secondary school, and a significant number of the pupils now continue in archery after leaving school.

Ben runs and coaches beginner's courses and provides further coaching to all ages and abilities, from ten years old up to eighty (and beyond!). His students are raw beginners up to Grand Master Bowman standard, and have competed at all levels except the Olympics—but there is still time!

CHECK OUT
OUR GREAT BOOKS

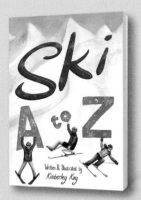

Kimberley Kay

SKI A TO Z

AN ILLUSTRATED GUIDE TO SKIING

This is a fun, illustrated introduction to skiing. Written and illustrated in the classic style of A-Z books, it provides valuable information and advice for anyone interested in skiing.

$14.95 US
Hardcover, 6.5 x 9.5", 112 p., in color
ISBN 978-1-78255-233-8

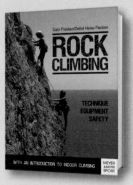

Flecken/Heise-Flecken

ROCK CLIMBING

TECHNIQUE | EQUIPMENT | SAFETY

This book will provide you with the right techniques, the crucial safety procedures, and the essential equipment needed to learn rock climbing. Numerous photos illustrate the challenging and complex movements.

$19.95 US
Paperback, 6.5 x 9.5", 216 p., in color
ISBN 978-1-78255-035-8

MEYER
& MEYER
SPORT

MEYER & MEYER Sport
Von-Coels-Str. 390
52080 Aachen
Germany

Phone   +49 02 41 - 9 58 10 - 13
Fax   +49 02 41 - 9 58 10 - 10
E-Mail   sales@m-m-sports.com
Website   www.m-m-sports.com

ALL ABOUT
OUTDOOR SPORTS

Witfeld/Gerling/Pach

THE ULTIMATE PARKOUR & FREERUNNING BOOK

This book contains precise illustrations for teaching all the basic techniques, easy-to-follow movement breakdowns, and methodical tips for indoor and outdoor training. It includes history, philosophy, rules of behavior, training advice, and interviews.

$19.95 US
Second Edition, Paperback, 6.5 x 9.5", 328 p., in color
ISBN 978-1-78255-020-4

Jeff Galloway

GALLOWAY'S 5K AND 10K RUNNING
TRAINING FOR RUNNERS & WALKERS

Olympian Jeff Galloway offers an easy method for training for a 5K or 10K. Using his proven Run Walk Run® method, you will gain control over fatigue while reducing or eliminating aches and pains.

$16.95 US
Fourth Edition, Paperback, 6.5 x 9.5", 200 p., in color
ISBN 978-1-78255-206-2

All information subject to change. © Adobe Stock

MEYER & MEYER Sport
Von-Coels-Str. 390
52080 Aachen
Germany

Phone +49 02 41 - 9 58 10 - 13
Fax +49 02 41 - 9 58 10 - 10
E-Mail sales@m-m-sports.com
Website www.m-m-sports.com

MEYER & MEYER SPORT

CREDITS

Cover and interior design: Anja Elsen

Layout: DiTech Publishing Services, www.ditechpubs.com

Cover photo: © AdobeStock

Chapter opener image: © AdobeStock

Interior images and photos: Courtesy of Ben Hastings

Managing editor: Elizabeth Evans

Copy editor: Anne Rumery